FAVORITE SHORT TRIPS IN NEW YORK STATE

A YANKEE BOOKS TRAVEL GUIDE

FAVORITE SHORT TRIPS IN NEW YORK STATE

by Harriet Webster

YANKEE BOOKS

For Deborah, who's doing much better than she realizes.
With affection and admiration.

Printed in the United States of America

Cover design by Dale Swensson
Interior design by Jill Shaffer

Library of Congress Catalog Card Number: 85-51872
ISBN 0-89909-090-7 paperback

Distributed in the book trade by St. Martin's Press

2   4   6   8   10   9   7   5   3   paperback

Contents

NANCIE BATTAGLIA

It's smooth sailing all the way on Mirror Lake in the village of Lake Placid.

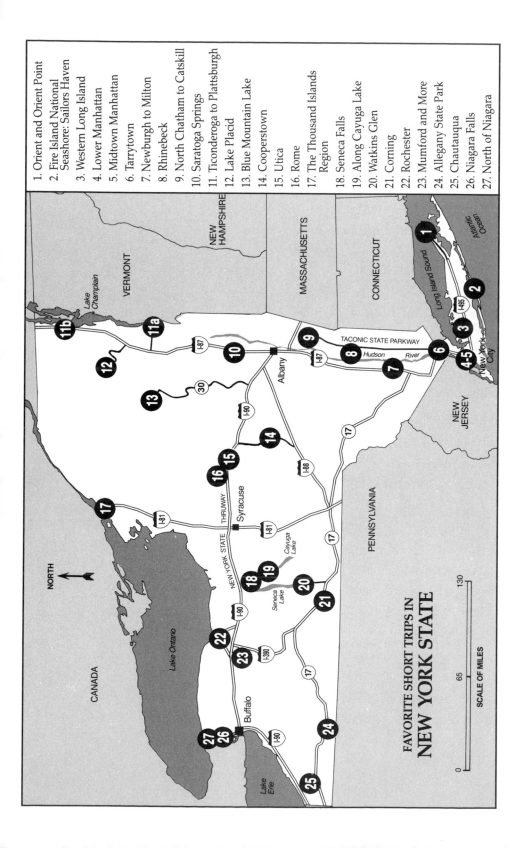

1. Orient and Orient Point
2. Fire Island National Seashore: Sailors Haven
3. Western Long Island
4. Lower Manhattan
5. Midtown Manhattan
6. Tarrytown
7. Newburgh to Milton
8. Rhinebeck
9. North Chatham to Catskill
10. Saratoga Springs
11. Ticonderoga to Plattsburgh
12. Lake Placid
13. Blue Mountain Lake
14. Cooperstown
15. Utica
16. Rome
17. The Thousand Islands Region
18. Seneca Falls
19. Along Cayuga Lake
20. Watkins Glen
21. Corning
22. Rochester
23. Mumford and More
24. Allegany State Park
25. Chautauqua
26. Niagara Falls
27. North of Niagara

FAVORITE SHORT TRIPS IN NEW YORK STATE

SCALE OF MILES

NORTH

Introduction

I grew up in New York City and, later, on Long Island. For me, "New York" has always been synonymous with Manhattan. Sure, my parents sometimes took me to visit relatives "upstate." They lived on a dairy farm in Amenia, about two hours north of New York City. And we visited friends "upstate" in New Paltz, even closer to the city. They lived on a farm, too, a gentleman's farm with lots of lovely horses to ride. It always amazed me that "upstate" was part of the same New York that my favorite city belonged to. It seemed somehow ludicrous to imagine these two farms in any way associated with *my* New York.

In the course of logging 15,000 miles on the highways and backroads of New York State while researching this book, I changed my tune. I was amazed at the thousands of acres of forested and open land that make up much of New York, the biggest of the northeastern states. Although it contains the largest metropolis in the country, New York is very much a rural state. And while Manhattan will always be special to me, I now know that there's a lot more to New York than a city, and a lot more to "upstate" than Amenia and New Paltz.

This is a book about traveling in New York State. The material is divided into a series of short trips, and the book is organized in an east-to-west fashion. While some of the trips fit neatly into a single day, others are better accomplished in a weekend or maybe even a week. I hope that you will string trips together to come up with an itinerary suited to your own tastes and time constraints. To make that easy, the map opposite shows all the destinations covered in the book and their geographic locations relative to one another. If you visit Rome, for example, you can easily extend your trip by spending a day in Utica, or perhaps by venturing a few miles farther to Seneca Falls.

I've followed the same basic pattern used in researching the other titles in the Yankee Guidebook series. I began by checking out the main attractions of a particular area, and then I started scouting the nearby towns. I talked to local people and tried to find out what they particularly like about where they live. It was Ann Sepe at Misty Meadow Hog Farm, for instance, who tipped me off to a couple of small, family-owned vineyards just

Many hands make light work. Preparing a meal at the Genesee Country Museum in Mumford.

down the road from her place. I encourage you to do the same on your next excursion — talk to the people you meet along the way, ask for their suggestions, and share your own discoveries.

There is so much to see and do in New York State that this book is just a beginning. The coverage is purposefully selective rather than comprehensive. (Better to say a lot about a limited number of places, I feel, than just to scratch the surface on a lot of different trips.) Most importantly, I've tried hard to convey a sense of the real feeling or spirit of each of the destinations we've included. Enjoy your travels throughout the state, but don't get so carried away with the variety and immensity that you forget about the Big Apple. It's still a first-class, fascinating city. And even if you've never been there, I think my two trip suggestions will make it an easy frontier to explore.

On a practical note, keep in mind that it's always important to call ahead and verify details if you have your heart set on visiting a particular attraction or participating in a specific activity. You want to be certain it's going to be open or operating when you get there. Another practical point is that the length of the write-up a trip receives should in no way dictate how long you'll want to stay. Lots of people spend weeks at Blue Mountain Lake (pages 85–89), while most visitors spend only a day or two in Cooperstown (pages 90–95).

Whether you're an athlete or an artist, a naturalist or a history buff, you'll find plenty here to satisfy your curiosity. The book covers activities that vary from philosophy lectures at the Chautauqua Institution to canoe trips in the Adirondacks, from industrial tours to cross-country skiing to craft workshops. Whether you prefer to explore famous Revolutionary battlefields or expansive wildflower gardens, you can do it all in New York State. There are some trips here especially for avid sightseers and others that are best suited to outdoorsmen. I've tried to offer diversity, both within the trips and between them, and I'm certain you'll find some that are just right for you.

Orient and Orient Point

JUDY AHRENS/THE SUFFOLK TIMES

One of the best ways to discover Orient Beach State Park — on two wheels and with a friend.

Only a hundred miles distant from the ultimate urban experience, New York City, the eastern part of Long Island might just as well be a galaxy removed; it is altogether another world. At Riverhead, the fish-shaped island divides sharply into a tail, the two skinny flukes (known as the North and South Forks) embracing the Great Peconic Bay and, farther out, Gardiners Bay. The tiny village of Orient sits on a peninsula near the end of the North Fork. The outermost tip of the fork is called Orient Point.

To reach the village you'll drive past ponds and fields of corn and potatoes, past vineyards and a parade of farmstands. Getting there in this case is very much part of the fun, so be sure to allow time along the way for a stop or two, perhaps to tour a fledgling Long Island winery or to pick your own strawberries at one of the many farms welcoming visitors in June. Come to Orient to walk and to enjoy the serenity of an unspoiled rural setting with the scent of salt water always in the air. Don't come

for nightlife or fancy boutiques. Such pleasures are best pursued in other places.

The community of Orient occupies about 3,000 acres, with the village located on the southwestern side of the fork overlooking Orient Bay. The area was originally called Oysterponds, a tribute to the wealth of oysters found in nearby waters, and was permanently settled in the mid-17th century. Indian tribes occupied the fork beginning nearly 700 years earlier, and over 30 Corchaug campsites have been identified in Orient.

Continuing several miles beyond the turnoff to the village, you come to the entrance of **Orient Beach State Park.** Here is a state park unlike any other we have visited. The entrance road borders Gardiners Bay, and if you come in the warm months you'll likely look out over a vista dotted with soaring seabirds and billowing white sails. Four miles long, the narrow spit runs southwest from the North Fork proper. The park has a lovely swimming beach, facing out on the open water where the bay meets Block Island Sound. We visited on a hot August Saturday and found the stretch of sand sparsely populated, a far cry from the crowded beaches associated with many public parks. The secret, we think, is that no one just happens to pass by this park. It's not really convenient to anywhere — you really have to want to come.

The swimming beach is sparsely populated — a far cry from the crowded sands of many public parks.

There is a ballfield, a refreshment stand (that also sells kites), and a bathhouse where you can change your clothes. There is also playground equipment — swings, slides, and seesaws. That's just about it for facilities. Saltwater fishing is permitted, but you'll need to bring along all your equipment, including bait. Come to Orient Point in the summer to picnic, swim, and lie in the sun. Come all year round to walk.

Take a hike along the beach, wandering inland when you see a trail. You'll come to the "red road," a clay road that leads out to an old foundation. Scrub pine covers much of the interior of the spit, and there are also two ponds, which attract water birds. Keep an eye out for terns, mockingbirds, maybe even an osprey. Because the tip of the island is located on the Atlantic Flyway, many varieties of birds stop off on their seasonal migrations. The spit is so narrow that it's pretty much impossible to get lost (you're never more than a few minutes from the salt water on either side), yet you will feel a million miles removed from civilization. It's about two and a half miles from the parking area to the end of the

spit if you choose to go all the way, but short walks are rewarding too.

Take your car on the Cross Sound Ferry from New London to Orient Point and leave the driving to your captain.

A few yards east of the park entrance sits the Orient Point terminal of the **Cross Sound Ferry,** which sails daily from Orient Point to New London, Connecticut. The ferry provides a pleasant access route for New Englanders who want to visit Long Island. The crossing takes about an hour and a half. Be certain to make reservations in advance if you want to take your car across. Bicyclists can leave their cars in New London, take their bikes across, and visit the state park and the village, returning home by ferry the same day. The flat, rural countryside offers ideal biking territory.

Let's turn now to the village of Orient. If you're hungry, you'll want to stop in at **The Orient Country Store,** which dates back to the days, as the owner explains, "when people did business in shillings and pounds." Today the store sells groceries and newspapers and has a delicatessen section. Order a sandwich at the small counter, or put together a picnic lunch and find a pretty spot to eat it outdoors. Unlike most businesses in the village, the store is open year round.

The Orient Country Store dates back to the days when people did business in shillings and pounds.

Just a few yards away, **The Ice Cream Works** also has a venerable, though far more recent, history. Back in 1926, the only ice cream parlor in town burnt to the ground right at the start of summer. With the help of volunteers, "Uncle" Ed King, an Orient farmer and entrepreneur, pieced together a small building in just six weeks, so that a new ice cream parlor could open in time for the Fourth of July. Although the parlor has seen renovation in the last half century, the original marble soda fountain counter is still in service, backed by the same wall of mirrors that Uncle Ed installed. Pretty apple-shaped jars of pink-colored water, each containing a few sprigs of Queen Anne's lace, sat on each of the seven tables the day we visited.

There are milk shakes (try the mocha), ice cream sodas, floats, and sundaes ("Chocolate Walnut Decadence" is a standout). If you want lunch first, you can order a magnificent hot dog from the umbrella-covered hot dog cart situated right in the middle of the ice cream parlor. These hefty all-beef franks (five to a pound) are served on sourdough buns with Dijon mustard, sauerkraut, red pepper relish, ketchup, and Manhattan onion sauce, in any combination you desire.

For a bit of post-refreshment shopping, browse in the **Old Orchard Farm Store,** again just a few yards away. Displayed on shelves and in baskets, and on old stoves like a 1920s enameled range (the proprietor collects them), are bottles of seasoned vinegars and marinades. Herbs are a specialty here, grown just up the road at the proprietor's in-laws' farm. They're sold fresh and dried, and there's a cart outside where you can select a clump of bush basil, silver thyme, or whatever you fancy to take home for your garden or windowsill. There are sweet-smelling soaps and bundles of potpourri, as well as small antiques like the old kitchen tools we saw.

"Chocolate Walnut Decadence" is a standout among all the shakes, sodas, floats, and sundaes.

If you love quilts, you'll want to make a stop at **Once Upon a House, Inc.,** a small shop just packed with handmade quilts in traditional and original patterns. Proprietor Sheila Zuhusky sends much of the work out to seasoned Amish and Mennonite quilters, as well as to talented needleworkers in Nova Scotia. The quilts hang on racks from ceiling to floor and over swinging bars. Some are pieced, others appliquéd. In addition to full-size quilts, there are shelves filled with wall hangings, baby bumpers, and lovely baby quilts. Special orders are welcome. If you have always wanted to make your own quilt but have never gotten around to it, you might find the answer here. You can purchase a pieced top and do the quilting yourself.

When you've finished exploring the shops, cross the street and visit the **Oysterponds Historical Society,** actually a collection of seven buildings, all within walking distance of one another. You'll begin in the Village House, which was built around 1790. A former inn and stagecoach stop, in the 1830s the house served as the home of one Augustus Griffin — local historian, schoolteacher, lobsterman, politician, storekeeper, poet, real estate broker, innkeeper, and auctioneer. Today it is furnished to reflect the Victorian period. A metal disc plays a polka on the formidable Olympia music box, setting the appropriate mood as you examine the parlor, with its needlepoint chair seats, floral carpets, and red velvet brocade curtains. Period accessories include a lidded Chinese tea basket with pink, silk-lined compartments for teapot and cups, and a glass dome over an arrangement of stuffed birds. The "Orient Room" contains items of local interest like the 1888 Orient Point Inn guest register and the willow basket used for more than a century to carry communion bread to the Congregational church.

Upstairs you'll find collections of old toys, including a large model of a locomotive, tender, and passenger coach built by a North Fork boy named Orrin F. Payne. He spent years working on it and finished in 1881. Take a peek through the lace-curtained windows of the yellow coach and you'll see passengers with china heads sitting in the red seats. Another upstairs room is devoted to "The Five Midgets of Oysterponds," members of the Tuthill family who lived here from the mid-1700s to the mid-1800s. Addison Tuthill was even smaller than the famous Tom Thumb. P.T. Barnum tried to persuade him to join the circus, but Addison opted instead for the quiet rural life. There is something genuinely touching about the tiny gloves, bonnets, and furniture that belonged to the family.

Addison Tuthill was even smaller than Tom Thumb. P.T. Barnum asked him to join the circus, but Tuthill opted for the quiet rural life.

JUDY AHRENS/THE SUFFOLK TIMES

Fifers parade and drummers keep the beat on 18th-Century Day at the Oysterponds Historical Society.

Some of the historical society's finest treasures live in the Webb House, built as an inn in 1720. (No, George Washington didn't sleep here, but he did stop in briefly for tea en route from Virginia to Boston.) The building was transported to its present location, overlooking Orient Bay, from neighboring Greenport in 1955. It was first moved by highway and then loaded onto a barge. The weight of the seven fireplaces and the huge chimneys made the barge sink deep into the mud. And there it all sat for several weeks, until the advent of a perigee moon produced a tide high enough to continue the journey. With its central doorway and generous verandah, the house has gracious proportions. There are two large rooms on each side of the entrance hall, both upstairs and down, with a single-story summer kitchen attached behind. The winter kitchen has both built-in and free-standing cupboards, while the summer kitchen boasts a brick hearth that takes up a whole wall. A Regina music box played "My Old Kentucky Home" as we admired the house and its furnishings. From the stair landing you can get a close-up look at the sailing ship weathervane perched atop the kitchen roof.

George Washington didn't sleep here, but he did stop in briefly en route to Boston.

The complex also includes the Old Point Schoolhouse, the Hallock Building (with its collection of ship models, maritime artifacts, and paintings), the Amanda Brown Schoolhouse, and the Red Barn (containing some fine old horsedrawn carriages alongside a penny candy counter where you can satisfy your sweet tooth). Shinbone Alley, which used to be the home of an Orient fisherman, now sits neatly behind its white fence and houses a consignment antiques shop, the proceeds from which benefit the historical society. Upstairs and down, room after room, it's packed with antiques and collectibles, the modest and the grand. Just poking through the eclectic offerings is lots of fun.

While you are visiting Orient, you might want to make a stop, coming or going, at one of the North Fork wineries. **Pindar Vineyards,** located on the north side of Route 25, began planting classic vinifera wine grapes in 1979 and now cultivates about 140 acres. The vines produce some 50,000 gallons of vinifera varietal and cuvée wines annually. Guided tours of the vineyard and winery are given on weekends. Weekday visitors are treated to a "video tour." All adult visitors have the opportunity to sample Pindar wines and, of course, wines are available for purchase. In the fall, you can also purchase fresh table grapes to take home. Pindar is only about a 20-minute drive from Orient, and a visit provides an excellent beginning or conclusion to your day on the North Fork.

ACCESS

ORIENT. Follow the Long Island Expressway, Route 495, east to its terminus in Riverhead. Follow signs to Route 25 east and continue to Orient.

ORIENT BEACH STATE PARK. Directions: Continue east on Route 25 from Orient to park entrance, on your right. **Season:** Year round. Closed Tuesday all year, and also Wednesdays from Columbus Day to Memorial Day. **Admission:** Charged. **Telephone:** (516) 323-2440.

CROSS SOUND FERRY SERVICE. Directions: Follow Route 25 to its end at Orient Point. You will be at the ferry terminal. **Season:** Year round. **Admission:** Charged. **Telephone:** For vehicle reservations departing from Orient Point call (516) 323-2743. For vehicle reservations departing from New London call (203) 443-5281.

THE ORIENT COUNTRY STORE. Directions: Located at 930 Village Lane in Orient. **Season:** Year round. **Admission:** Free. **Telephone:** (516) 323-2580.

THE ICE CREAM WORKS. Directions: Located at 1010 Village Lane in Orient. **Season:** Daily, late June through Labor Day. Weekends in May and early June and September through November. **Admission:** Free. **Telephone:** (516) 323-3602.

OLD ORCHARD FARM STORE. Directions: Located on Village Lane in Orient. **Season:** Open Wednesday through Sunday, May through December. **Admission:** Free. **Telephone:** None.

ONCE UPON A HOUSE, INC. Directions: Located on Village Lane in Orient. **Season:** Mid-June to Labor Day, and other times by appointment. **Admission:** Free. **Telephone:** (516) 323-3575.

OYSTERPONDS HISTORICAL SOCIETY. Directions: Follow Route 25 to Orient. Turn right on Village Lane and you will see the main building, the Village House, on your left. **Season:** Tuesday through Sunday afternoons in July and August. Weekend afternoons in June and September. **Admission:** Charged. **Telephone:** (516) 323-2480.

PINDAR VINEYARDS. Directions: Located on Route 25 in Peconic. **Season:** Memorial Day weekend through December 31. **Admission:** Free. **Telephone:** (516) 734-6200.

For lodging and restaurant suggestions in the area, write to the Greenport-Southold Chamber of Commerce at P.O. Box 66, Greenport, N.Y. 11944. **Telephone:** (516) 477-1383.

JUDY AHRENS/THE SUFFOLK TIMES

In vino veritas? *Dr. Herodotus Damianos, owner of Pindar Vineyards, does some impromptu modeling at his roadside stand.*

Fire Island National Seashore: Sailors Haven

A skinny finger of land, extending 32 miles from east to west, Fire Island buffers the Great South Bay and the Long Island mainland from the full force of the Atlantic Ocean. Folks from New York City and many busy Long Island communities flock to this barrier island's 17 communities during the summer months, seeking respite in an environment free from cars, with the exception of the jeeps and other small vehicles that serve as fire engines, police cars, and garbage trucks. They come to swim and to bike, to walk and to jog, and to generally get away from it all. While the communities here vary in character — some are family oriented, others cater more to the lively singles scene; some boast wall-to-wall boutiques, others rely on a single general store — they all provide an opportunity to experience the sun, sand, and salty air.

Many of these communities, however, are not really accessible to day visitors. You can get to them, but once you're there you won't find public facilities. Fire Island National Seashore is another story. Operated by the National Park Service, the national seashore includes four separate areas. Our favorite is the Sailors Haven section. To get there, you'll enjoy a half-hour ferry ride across Great South Bay, courtesy of the **Sunken Forest Ferry Company.** Take a seat on the enclosed lower deck or find a spot out in the open on the upper deck and get a head start on your tan, as you glide past the sailboats and motorboats in the bay. Be certain to bring along a bathing suit, a towel, and a sweatshirt for the return trip, when the air cools down at the end of the day. You might even want to bring fishing gear, or perhaps a picnic.

Folks from the city flock to Fire Island during the summer, seeking respite in a car-free environment.

An almost circus-like atmosphere pervades Sailors Haven on a warm summer day. The blue and white ferry pulls in, dropping off a cheerful parade of visitors. Forest rangers in dark green shorts and gray shirts patiently answer questions in the **Visitor Center,** where little kids go "yuck" at the crusty tube worm on the "touch me" table. Early in the morning, visitors enthusiastically tackle plates of pancakes on the open deck by the **snack bar,** shaded by large umbrellas. Later in the day, the

You never know what strange sea creatures may turn up in the seine nets at Fire Island National Seashore.

menu shifts to chiliburgers and fried shrimp, washed down with beer or wine. And, no matter what the hour, someone's likely to be licking an ice cream cone. The adjacent gift shop rents beach umbrellas, not a bad idea if you're thinking of a whole day out in the sun.

If you're interested in nature programs, check the schedule in the Visitor Center as soon as you arrive. Sample programs include the opportunity to build an absolutely stupendous communal sand castle with the assistance of a forest ranger well versed in the finer points of seaweed, sand, shell, and driftwood decoration. Rangers also take children seining in the bay. Using nets they haul up and examine all sorts of crabs, fish, and snails. Guided tours of the Sunken Forest occur every afternoon during the summer. More about the forest later.

Sailors Haven also has a **marina,** for those who arrive by boat. There are 36 slips available, and visitors are permitted to stay up to seven consecutive days. Call the Visitor Center for additional information. Adjacent to the slips, you'll find picnic tables and grills overlooking the bay, which you are free to use whether you've come by ferry or private boat. Other facilities include cold showers and changing rooms, convenient if you want to wash off

Build a communal sand castle with the help of a forest ranger well versed in driftwood decor.

the salt before heading home. There is a bay swimming area, but we much prefer to lug our paraphernalia down to the oceanside, where the surf beats against the broad, sandy beach, backed by the dunes and the Sunken Forest. Don't be surprised if you see a forest ranger riding a horse through the froth at the edge of the beach.

Varying in width from a quarter of a mile to just a few hundred feet, Fire Island contains a fascinating mixture of natural environments. There are wet sections and dry sections, windblown and sheltered. In some parts of the island vegetation thrives, while in others almost nothing seems to grow. At Sailors Haven, you can explore one of these environments in the form of a 300-year-old maritime holly forest. Here you will learn to identify plants and to appreciate the complex web of relationships that exists between a specific habitat and the forms of life it supports. What makes this part of the island so special is the Sunken Forest, a dense expanse of trees, bushes, and vines nestled down behind the high dunes, which offer protection from the harsh battering of the sea.

At the Visitor Center, you can buy an inexpensive booklet that provides a guided tour of the forest. The "trail" is actually a network of well-tended, easily traversed boardwalks (wear footgear to avoid splinters). Although the boardwalk is only a little less than a mile and a half in length, you should allow at least an hour for the walk, giving yourself plenty of time to find the 35 features identified in the booklet. Do be alert for the clumps of poison ivy that thrive on the island. The old saying, "Leaflets three, let it be," makes a lot of sense here.

With the help of the booklet and numbered spots along the boardwalk, you'll locate the shadbush (sometimes called juneberry or shadblow) by its striped, light gray bark, and the sassafras by its deeply ridged, reddish-brown covering. You'll find sour gum trees in the boggy areas and American holly, a sizable evergreen with twisted limbs and sharply pointed green leaves, out in the open. Bearberry, a thick, low, evergreen "rug," is easiest to spot in the spring, when it has white flowers, or toward the end of the summer, when it flaunts small red berries.

As you explore the forest you'll come to high rises, where you'll notice that the tops of the vegetation are almost uniformly level. This is because, while the ocean salt provides nutrients for the forest, it can also destroy foliage when it is highly

Bearberry is easy to spot in the spring, when it has white flowers, or in late summer, when it flaunts small red berries.

concentrated. As branches stretch higher into the air, above the protection of the dunes, they reach a level of salt concentration so intense that it kills rather than nourishes. So when the foliage reaches the height of the dunes, it begins to grow laterally instead of vertically and forms a leafy roof over the forest floor. You'll feel as though you are walking in a dark, cool passage beneath a delicate canopy. As we walked, we came across a group of scientists using sophisticated gadgetry to measure the amount of water in sassafras leaves. One of them warned us not to chew on the leaves — "They're carcinogenic. . . ." Of course, we had already read warnings not to pick any of the plants in this fragile environment.

If you should land on this boardwalk, the only way to "Go" passes through the surreal and beautiful Sunken Forest.

Many birds and animals make their homes in the forest, and the more unobtrusive you are, the more likely you are to get a glimpse of them. A white-tailed deer trotted briskly through the brush not far from the boardwalk as we hiked through, and some people we encountered later on along the trail were ecstatic because they'd just spotted a fox. Mice and rabbits are frequent sights and weasels sometimes appear. If you're a birdwatcher, you'll want to bring along binoculars, since sightings of yellow-bellied sapsuckers, black-capped chickadees, eastern wood peewees, and brown thrashers are common.

As you follow the boardwalk, you'll find bench-edged platforms where you can stop to rest and enjoy the scenery. There are a few elevated spots where the vista provides glimpses of both ocean and bay, particularly as you approach Sailors Haven on the return part of the loop. The boardwalk includes several ramps and four sets of steps.

A visit to Sailors Haven and the Sunken Forest offers an opportunity to sample the natural beauty of this fragile barrier island with a minimum of fuss. Leave your car behind on the mainland and use your feet as transportation for the day. Hike, swim, picnic, and become acquainted with a beautiful place. What better way to pass a summer day!

ACCESS

FIRE ISLAND NATIONAL SEASHORE: SAILORS HAVEN. To reach Sailors Haven, take the Sunken Forest Ferry from Sayville, N.Y. Can also be reached by private boat.

SUNKEN FOREST FERRY COMPANY. Directions: Coming from the west to Sayville, take the Long Island

Expressway (Route 495) east to Exit 59 south. Turn right at the first light onto Ocean Avenue (Route 93). Take Route 93 south for 6.5 miles to eighth light (Route 93 ends at fifth light, but continue straight on Lakeland Avenue). At eighth light, which is at corner of Main Street in Sayville, follow green-and-white "Fire Island Ferry" signs to terminal. **Season:** Early May through October. **Admission:** Charged. **Telephone:** (516) 589-8980.

SAILORS HAVEN VISITOR CENTER. Directions: Located at the ferry dock in Sailors Haven. **Season:** Weekdays from the end of April through November 1; weekends also from mid-May to the end of September. **Admission:** Free. **Telephone:** (516) 597-6183.

SAILORS HAVEN CONCESSION. Directions: Located at the ferry dock in Sailors Haven. **Season:** Early May to mid-October. **Admission:** Free. **Telephone:** None.

MARINA. Directions: Located at the ferry dock in Sailors Haven. **Season:** Early May to mid-October. **Admission:** Fees charged. **Telephone:** Call Visitor Center for information.

ADDITIONAL SERVICES. Showers, changing rooms, rest room facilities, pay phone, and use of nature trail are available from late April to mid-October, all in the area of the ferry dock in Sailors Haven. Interpretive programs originate at the Visitor Center and take place from the end of June through Labor Day. Lifeguards are on duty at the swimming beach from the end of June through Labor Day. There are no fees for any of these services. Call the Visitor Center for additional information.

Western Long Island

OLD BETHPAGE VILLAGE RESTORATION

A new broom sweeps clean the general store at Old Bethpage Village Restoration.

J ust an hour's drive from New York City, western Long Island offers a tranquil quartet of gracious attractions. The three estates and the restored village described here share a serenity that contrasts sharply with the frenzied tempo of the traffic snarls and busy shopping centers you'll encounter in getting to them. Don't try to visit all four places in one trip; choose one or two, and save the others for another time. Each one has too much to offer to be treated in a hurry.

Built by Theodore Roosevelt in 1884–85, Sagamore Hill in Oyster Bay was to remain the famous statesman's home for the rest of his life. T.R. moved into the house with his sister and his infant daughter Alice (his first wife having died only hours after Alice's birth). In 1886, he married a childhood friend, Edith Kermit Carow, and here they raised their family, which grew to include five more children. "There could be no healthier and pleasanter place in which to bring up children than in that

nook of old-time America around Sagamore Hill," reflected Roosevelt. "Certainly I never knew small people to have a better time or a better training for their work in afterlife than . . . at Sagamore Hill."

Now known as the **Sagamore Hill Historic Site,** the estate was named for Sagamore Mohannis, the Indian chief who signed away rights to the land more than two centuries earlier. Devoted to tough physical challenges and the outdoor life, Roosevelt joined his children here in playing games, chopping wood, riding horseback, and hiking in the woods. Throughout his career — from president of the Police Commission of New York City to assistant secretary of the Navy, lieutenant colonel in the Rough Riders to governor of New York, vice president to president of the United States — Roosevelt always returned home to Sagamore Hill.

A solid, rambling, Victorian frame-and-brick house with yellow shingles and dark green shutters, Sagamore Hill today looks much as it did when the Roosevelts lived here; its 23 rooms are filled with family possessions. A hostess stands ready to answer your questions, but you can either wander through the three floors independently or rent a recorded tour in the gift shop, to listen to as you explore the house.

Children are awed by the arched elephant tusks and the lion and leopard rugs.

Children are awed by the great arched elephant tusks and the lion and leopard rugs in the north room, where a hunting hat and binoculars hang casually from a set of antlers mounted on the wall. On the second floor you'll see the family bedrooms and the guest rooms, and on the third floor you'll visit the maids' rooms and a room referred to as a "giant playpen," which was, according to one of the Roosevelt daughters, "used for children who had outgrown the nursery but still had to be contained." You'll also see the schoolroom where the children took their lessons.

Walking the spacious grounds, you'll come across the wooden windmill that was used to pump water for the house. Lemon lilies, roses, and a rainbow of annuals grow in the garden spaces used by the family to raise flowers and vegetables. In the carriage house, you'll get a glimpse of some of T.R.'s vehicles, which included a surrey, phaeton, pony cart, three-seat carriage, and an old wooden farm wagon fitted with wooden runners for sleigh rides. Take a short walk, past aging apple trees, to Orchard Museum, a part of the historic site. Here you will see a film about Theodore Roosevelt's life. Narrated by Mike Wallace and illustrated with photographs and news clips, the film is a lively biography chronicling the high points in his long career of public service. You'll listen to T.R.'s sage words on the eve of his first presidential election: "We are a great people and we must play a great part in the world. All that we must decide is whether we will play it well or ill." You can also browse in the two galleries, which are filled with family photos and memorabilia varying from son Kermit's tiny red leather buckle shoes to T.R.'s swords.

Also in Oyster Bay, you can visit **Planting Fields Arboretum.** The former estate of the late William Robertson Coe is divided into 40 acres of lawn, 160 acres of arboretum, and about 200 acres of woodlands and fields. There is also a large complex of greenhouses where you'll see tropical and subtropical vegetation including orchids, hibiscus, ferns, bromeliads, begonias, palms, cacti, and pineapple plants, as well as coffee, cocoa, banana, and citrus trees. One greenhouse is devoted entirely to camellias, over a hundred varieties of them, which bloom in the winter. The conservatory greenhouse features cyclamen and poinsettias in the winter, English garden annuals and Easter lilies in the spring. Bedding plants like begonias and impatiens predominate in the summer, with orchids and chrysanthemums stealing the limelight in the fall.

Joe and Harold, the resident macaws, show off their striking plumage while saying typically bird-brain things.

While visiting the main greenhouse, be sure to stop by for a few words with Joe and Harold, the resident macaws. They say typically bird-brain things like "I am a good boy. I am a bad, bad bird," while showing off their striking red, green, blue, and yellow plumage.

The rhododendron and azalea collections at Planting Fields are among the finest in the East. Peak bloom occurs from mid-April to mid-June. Other special areas include the formal gardens, the rose arbor, the wildflower garden, the heather garden, the dwarf conifer garden, and the day lily garden. Along the driveways and lawns, you'll see beech, linden, elm, cedar, and tulip trees, as well as the magnolia and maple collections and the holly plantings.

If you visit on a Tuesday, Wednesday, or Thursday afternoon between April and September, you can take a guided tour of Coe Hall. The 65-room house, built in 1921 to replace the original dwelling (which was destroyed by fire), is considered one of the finest examples of Tudor architecture in the country. If you visit at another time, you can pick up a guide to the exterior of the building at the bookstore. The pamphlet describes details of the Indian limestone mansion, like the decorative shield with the storm-tossed ship that sits over the main entrance. (Mr. Coe was quite a success in the marine insurance business.)

From the end of June to early September each year, the **Friends of the Arts Summer Festival** is held under a tent on the grounds of Planting Fields. The eclectic schedule is likely to include everything from an evening with the Preservation Hall Jazz Band to a Beethoven festival. Write ahead for program and ticket information.

Dolls and stuffed bears celebrate a birthday in the elegant playhouse.

Another Long Island estate well worth a leisurely visit is **Old Westbury Gardens,** a private residence built in the early 20th century to re-create the ambiance of an 18th-century English country estate. Garden lovers will rejoice at the splendid formal gardens and the meticulous landscaping. Stroll down "avenues" lined with beech and linden trees, across open lawns, and along the edges of ponds, where Canada geese make themselves at home. Take the primrose path through the rose garden, then continue on to our favorite place, the walled garden. Fountains, statuary, a goldfish pond, secluded benches where young lovers embrace — not to mention the wealth of blooms — all combine to make this an appealing and romantic spot.

We also loved the cottage garden. Here you can peek into the elegant playhouse, where dolls and

The magnificent house and grounds at Old Westbury Gardens re-create an 18th-century English country estate.

stuffed bears are celebrating a birthday. If there are children in your entourage, they will enjoy playing in the sandboxes (where else can you dig surrounded by rose trellises?) and in the three log cabins that sit nearby. Lots of people bring a good book along, so they can simply sit in the gardens and enjoy themselves as long as they please. This is not a place for hurrying! Feel free to bring a picnic lunch to spread out on the ample lawn, or you might want to purchase lunch at the snack bar, prettily set in a wooded grove with picnic tables nearby.

Children will enjoy playing in the sandboxes. (Where else can you dig surrounded by rose trellises?)

The stately Stuart manor, Westbury House, poses elegantly at the center of the estate and is open to visitors. The motto above the door reads "Pax Introentibus — Salus Exeuntibus," or "Peace to those who enter, good health to those who leave." The interior of the house looks much the same as it did 75 years ago, when it was the home of Mr. and Mrs. John S. Phipps. The house contains paintings by artists such as John Singer Sargent, Thomas Gainsborough, and Joshua Reynolds. The conservatory, with its abundance of glass and pink-and-mauve-flowered couches and chairs, made us want to move right in. In addition to a collection of fine English antiques, there are serendipitous personal and architectural touches throughout the house — Mr. Phipps' walnut-and-mahogany wheelchair, the naked statuary supporting the marble mantle in the dining room, the Chinese hand-painted wallpaper complete with flowers, parrots, and butterflies. All in all, the estate is an excellent example of Long Island elegance of another era.

Quite another facet of Long Island's past comes alive at **Old Bethpage Village Restoration.** A living-history museum re-creating 18th- and 19th-century rural life, the village documents the daily habits of early Long Island residents. Homes, barns, stores, and other buildings from that period have been moved here from their original sites and painstakingly restored. Today they are populated with costumed interpreters, who familiarize visitors with their domestic habits, social customs, and work styles. An orientation film is shown periodically in the reception center, providing background on the evolution of the village.

You'll walk down country lanes into the center of town and visit a farm where draft horses plow the fields and pigs wallow cheerfully in the mud. The lady of the house chops up vegetables to add to the pork ribs simmering over her open fire. The rug she is braiding sits nearby, awaiting attention. Outside, a cow stands belly deep in the pond, savoring the coolness.

In the general store you can play a game of checkers with playing pieces sliced from a dried-out corncob. Then admire the stock on the store shelves, including everything from an old leather baseball to a china doll, bonnets to beaded bags to bolts of fabric. There's even an example of the very first washing machine ever manufactured. This wooden contraption from 1861 testifies to the beginning rumblings of the Industrial Revolution in America.

In the general store you can play a game of checkers with pieces sliced from a dried-out corncob.

In the tavern, you can cash in the paper "scrip" you bought on entering the village. Purchase a glass of birch beer, a pretzel, or a stick of candy to eat at a wooden tavern table. Outside, under the trees, a basket maker and a broom maker are at work, while a visiting child tries her luck at rolling a wooden hoop. In the hat shop, the hatter demonstrates how felt hats were formed on wooden molds. A bowler or derby hat cost two dollars back in those days, about a week's salary for a farm hand. In the one-room schoolhouse, the schoolmaster gives visitors a taste of early education. There are currently 14 restored buildings open to the public, and the village is still growing.

Just as the tempo of rural life varied with the seasons, the pace at Old Bethpage Village reflects the progress of the calendar. There are seasonal and holiday events throughout the year, and it is certainly worthwhile to try and plan your visit to coincide with one of these. You might make sentimental valentines or celebrate Washington's Birthday in February. March is just right for a quilting bee, while August is the time for a game of 1860s-style baseball. Political campaigning, balloting, and victory celebrations (for the 1848 elections) characterize November. From May to early September, music awakens the village every weekend. A visit is a treat at any season of the year; just be sure to dress for the weather.

ACCESS

WESTERN LONG ISLAND. To reach western Long Island, travel east on the Long Island Expressway (Route 495). All sites listed below are easily accessible from the Expressway.

SAGAMORE HILL HISTORIC SITE. Directions: Follow the Long Island Expressway (Route 495) to Exit 441. Take Route 106 north to Oyster Bay. Turn right at the third

A performer stretches a few tall tales at Old Bethpage Village.

traffic light and follow signs. **Season:** Year round. **Admission:** Small charge. **Telephone:** (516) 922-4447.

PLANTING FIELDS ARBORETUM. Directions: Follow the Long Island Expressway (Route 495) to Exit 39N (Glen Cove Road). Travel north on Glen Cove Road to Route 25A. Turn right on Route 25A and continue east to Wolver Hollow Road (there's a police station on the corner). Turn left on Wolver Hollow Road. At intersection, bear right on Chicken Valley Road, then right on Planting Fields Road. Entrance will be on your right. **Season:** Year round. Coe Hall is open Tuesday, Wednesday, and Thursday afternoons from April through September. **Admission:** Charged. **Telephone:** (516) 922-9201.

FRIENDS OF THE ARTS SUMMER FESTIVAL. Directions: Performances are held at Planting Fields Arboretum. **Season:** Late June to early September. **Admission:** Charged. **Telephone:** (516) 922-0061.

OLD WESTBURY GARDENS. Directions: Follow the Long Island Expressway (Route 495) to Exit 39S (Glen Cove Road). Follow the service road for 1.2 miles. Turn right on Old Westbury Road and continue one-half mile to entrance. **Season:** Late April through October. **Admission:** Charged. (There is also a separate additional admission fee to enter the mansion.) **Telephone:** (516) 333-0048.

OLD BETHPAGE VILLAGE RESTORATION. Directions: Follow the Long Island Expressway (Route 495) to Exit 48; signs indicate the way to the village entrance from the exit. **Season:** Year round. **Admission:** Charged. **Telephone:** (516) 420-5280.

For lodging and restaurant suggestions in the western Long Island area, contact the Chamber of Commerce, 1776 Nichols Court, Hempstead, N.Y. 11550. **Telephone:** (516) 483-2000.

Lower Manhattan

Trade has always been a vital part of New York City's history, and a trip to lower Manhattan will introduce you to the lively tempo of commercial life, past and present. This part of the city fairly pulsates with activity on a weekday morning. You get the feeling that deals are being made wherever you turn, whether it be along the wharves of the restored 19th-century seaport or in the halls of the contemporary "twin towers." The streets are full of businesspeople toting attaché cases and munching on hot dogs, pretzels, or bags of gumdrops purchased from the street vendors who stake out nearly every corner.

To get your bearings, begin with a visit to the **Observation Deck at the World Trade Center.** Climb aboard the express elevator for a 58-second ride up to the 107th floor. Surrounded by floor-to-ceiling windows, the deck provides a 360-degree panorama of the city below. You'll see famous landmarks like the Brooklyn Bridge and the Statue of Liberty. You'll see skyscrapers and parks and tangles of traffic in the densely packed streets a quarter of a mile below.

The observation deck also contains an extensive exhibit called "To Market, To Market." It chronicles the role of items as diverse as cows, cowrie shells, and computers in the development of trade patterns and practices. The earliest trade goods were necessities like fuel, cloth, building materials, and food. And, of course, the types of objects traded reveal much about their owners' lifestyles. As 19th-century American orator Robert Ingersoll observed, "We exchange ideas when we exchange fabrics." The final section of the exhibit focuses on the future of trade. Demographers predict that there will be twice as many people on earth in the year 2000 as there were in 1960. The emphasis of trade is moving from goods to services, consistent with an old adage: "Give a man a fish and feed him for a day. Teach a man to fish and feed him for life."

When you have finished looking at the exhibit and peering out the windows, take an escalator ride up to the Rooftop Promenade, above the 110th floor. You'll be outside, standing on the world's highest observation platform. Watch the helicopters dart by below, as you stare down into a city of more than seven million people.

American orator Robert Ingersoll once observed, "We exchange ideas when we exchange fabrics."

When you leave the observation deck you'll probably want to explore the World Trade Center further. You might want to stop in at the Visitors' Gallery of the Commodities Exchange Center (ninth floor, Four World Trade Center), where you can watch dealers buy and sell gold, silver, coffee, sugar, and cotton at auction down on the trading floor. For shoppers, the World Trade Center Concourse is Manhattan's largest indoor shopping mall, containing more than 60 stores. You needn't go hungry either, because there are more than 22 restaurants in the World Trade Center. **The Big Kitchen,** which is actually eight different restaurants all in one, is lots of fun. It's a little like a street festival brought indoors, offering everything from egg rolls to oysters, barbecue to burgers — all self-service.

From the World Trade Center, take a brief walk to **Trinity Church.** (Pedestrian maps are clearly posted throughout this part of the city, making it easy to find your way from one site to another.) The third of three Trinity Church buildings at this location, the present church is a classic example of Gothic Revival architecture. When it was completed in 1846, its splendid spire dominated the lower New York skyline and became a comforting landmark for sailors entering New York Harbor. In 1705, Trinity conducted the first ministry to slaves and free blacks in New York City, and during the 19th century the church offered special ministries to meet the needs of the many thousands of immigrants pouring into the city from all over the world. In the Trinity Museum, adjoining the church, you'll see

Is this an Orwellian nightmare come true? Nope, just business as usual on the floor of the New York Stock Exchange.

artifacts, documents, maps, and photographs related to the church. A brief slide show provides an introduction to the exhibits and to the history of the parish.

Continue your walk, heading now to the **New York Stock Exchange.** The lobby contains several pushbutton exhibits. One teaches you how to read a stock table; another answers 20 commonly asked questions (What is meant by buying on margin? What is an odd lot?) in German, Spanish, French, or English. If you want to get an update on the status of your own financial holdings, you can call up price quotations on one of the three computer terminals set up for your convenience. Your hostess will give you a quick lesson on how to read "the tape," which runs overhead continuously during market hours, reflecting each of the 100 to 120 million transactions that take place on an average day.

Your hostess will give you a quick lesson on how to read "the tape," which runs overhead continuously during market hours.

An eight-minute slide show explains that the Exchange was formed by a group of 18th-century traders who had been involved in buying and selling government bonds to pay off Revolutionary War debts. Today more than 1,500 companies are traded on the Exchange. You'll learn how brokers execute orders and you'll become acquainted with some of the 11 major computer systems that keep track of those transactions. Then comes the best part of the visit — an opportunity to step into the Visitors' Gallery overlooking the floor of the famous New York Stock Exchange. It's hard to believe that the action taking place in the room below is the very same stuff that's reported on radio and television all over the country whenever a reporter says, "Today on Wall Street . . . ." Clerks in blue jackets mark orders on electronically sensitive cards, while women in suits and well-dressed businessmen with white badges confer seriously (they're actual traders). Guys in rolled-up shirtsleeves talk frantically on the telephones that seem to be everywhere. Numbers flash on the row of video display screens situated above each trading post. Meanwhile, in the gallery, a taped narration explains what's happening on the paper-strewn trading floor below, helping you to make sense of the frantic scene.

The nonstop action taking place below you is the very same stuff that's reported on radio and television all over the country.

For a change of pace, take a giant step back from the flash and dash and high-tension dealings of the 20th century. The **Fraunces Tavern Museum,** located upstairs from Fraunces Tavern (where George Washington bade farewell to his key officers at the end of the Revolution), interprets 18th-century American history and culture through its permanent collection of prints, paintings, and decorative arts. In addition to the galleries, there are two period rooms to visit. In the Clinton Dining Room, the table is set for the concluding course in a gentlemen's meal, with fruit knives, dessert plates, and glasses and decanters for sweet wine and brandy. The room is furnished in early 19th-century Duncan Phyfe furniture, and the intriguing wallpaper sports scenes from the American Revolution. Made in Alsace in 1838, the paper's design was handprinted with woodblocks.

The Long Room, where Washington said goodbye to his officers, is outfitted with 18th-century pieces and is arranged as a private dining room in which favored groups of men were permitted to meet. A round of "all fours," a popular Colonial card game, is spread out on one table, a long white clay pipe and a wad of tobacco on another. The sideboard holds a symmetrical display of nuts, jellies, and other treats, including a tower of red and green grapes sitting on a cake. There are a couple of spyglasses by the window, these being provided by early tavernkeepers so that their merchant customers could observe ships entering and leaving the harbor outside.

The museum offers a 10-minute audio-visual presentation, "A Colonial Seed Grows a Big Apple," which focuses on the early history of New York. A series of free lectures and demonstrations are offered during the week, covering topics like "Science and Witchcraft in Colonial Times" and "George Washington's Teeth: Dentistry in 18th-Century America." Call ahead for up-to-date information. If you would like to sample roast oysters or other delicious fare at Fraunces Tavern, be sure to make reservations well in advance. The Colonial-era inn is a favorite with visitors and businesspeople alike and is almost always filled to capacity at lunchtime.

Now head down to the **South Street Seaport Museum** at the base of Fulton Street. This extraordinary museum encompasses architectural landmarks, working boats, and historic vessels, as well as the famous Fulton Market and a piece of New York Harbor. You could easily spend a whole day here just exploring the shops tucked away in Schermerhorn Row, the seaport's architectural centerpiece. Its proximity to the sea transformed New York into a great city during the 17th and 18th centuries. By the 19th century, the port, based here on South Street, was operating at a feverish pace. Merchants and entrepreneurs slapped up new

FRAUNCES TAVERN MUSEUM

Dwarfed by today's financial giants, the Fraunces Tavern once catered to 18th-century merchants — and to George Washington, too.

warehouses and counting houses to handle the burgeoning volume of business transacted along the waterfront, as ships continually brought goods in and out of the city. The port hummed even more energetically with the opening of the Erie Canal in 1825, when produce and other goods from the Midwest began flowing into the harbor. Looking out over South Street and the piers in the 1830s, you would have seen trans-Atlantic packets, Caribbean schooners, and China clippers standing stern-to-stern alongside fishing smacks, Long Island Sound steamboats, and grain barges.

One way to get a taste of the past is to take in a showing of *The South Street Venture* at the Translux Seaport Theater, housed in a 1914-vintage building originally constructed as a fish-processing plant. Using over 100 projectors, 33 speakers, a 45-foot-long panoramic screen, and 31 auxiliary screens, this production makes you feel as though you're really there: back in the 19th century with the salt spray in your face as you travel around Cape Horn; right in the middle of a tremendous fire ravaging the seaport; or pulling out all the stops in a dance hall and downing a pint of grog. Over 150 special effects are incorporated into the show, making it a real hit with kids. From the crashing of masts to the boom of cannons, this spirited multimedia presentation is never the slightest bit dull.

You'll also want to visit Fulton Market, the fourth market to bear that name (this one constructed in 1983). There has been a market on this block ever since 1822. Butchers were the earliest tenants, followed by fish sellers, sausage stands, produce dealers, and dairy-goods vendors. Oyster stands, bookstalls, and cake stands came a little later. The new market re-creates the eclectic group of merchants that characterized the first Fulton Market. The cavernous building has an industrial feel, with red metal stair rails, tile floors, and towering ceilings. Dozens of pushcarts and stalls are accommodated inside, selling everything from fresh flowers to fresh shrimp, sweatshirts to ceramics. There are common eating areas where you can carry the pasta salad or Chinese food, Polish sausage or fresh fruit compote you've purchased at the food stands. Music plays, huge wooden fish hang suspended from the ceiling, and the whole atmosphere is festive and upbeat.

If you can tear yourself away, take some time to explore the *Peking*, a four-masted bark built in 1911 in Germany. Carrying more than an acre of sail, this

From the piers in the 1830s, you would have seen trans-Atlantic packets and China Clippers standing alongside fishing smacks and grain barges.

You can buy just about anything, from ceramics to salads, inside the venerable Fulton Market.

fast, trim vessel hauled general cargo from Europe to South America, returning filled with nitrate fertilizer for Europe's over-cultivated fields. Several staterooms, a seamen's forecastle, and the sailroom have already been re-created, and further restoration continues. A film depicting a stormy passage around Cape Horn, made aboard the *Peking* in 1929, is shown regularly.

You can also visit the *Wavertree*, a full-rigged British ship dating back to 1885, currently the largest iron-hulled sailing vessel preserved in any museum. Her early years were spent transporting jute from what is now Bangladesh to Britain, to be used for making rope and burlap. By 1888 she had gone into general "tramping," that is, taking aboard whatever cargoes she could find. In 1895, for example, she brought nitrate fertilizer from the west coast of South America to New York, then left for Calcutta loaded with canned kerosene.

We've only begun to scratch the surface of the South Street Seaport. Dedicated to preserving the city's maritime history, the complex also includes the Maritime Crafts Center, where model shipbuilding, wooden carving, and other maritime crafts are demonstrated. Be sure to check out the lightship *Ambrose*, the Museum Gallery, and Bowne & Co. Stationers, a re-created printer's and stationer's shop of the 1870s, where you can watch old-fashioned letterpress printing. Might as well just resign yourself to the fact that, no matter how much time you set aside for the Seaport, it probably won't be enough. You'll just have to come back.

OBSERVATION DECK AT THE WORLD TRADE CENTER. Directions: The trade center occupies the block bordered by West Side Drive, Vesey Street, Liberty Street, and Church Street in lower Manhattan. All three New York City subway systems — the IRT, BMT, and IND — stop at the trade center. **Season:** Year round. **Admission:** Charged. **Telephone:** (212) 466-7377.

THE BIG KITCHEN. Directions: Located on the Concourse in the World Trade Center. **Season:** Year round. **Admission:** Free. **Telephone:** (212) 938-1153.

TRINITY CHURCH. Directions: Located at the corner of Broadway and Wall Street. **Season:** Year round. **Admission:** Free. **Telephone:** (212) 602-0800.

NEW YORK STOCK EXCHANGE. Directions: The entrance to the Visitors' Gallery is located at 20 Broad Street, just off Wall Street. **Season:** Year round. **Admission:** Free. **Telephone:** (212) 623-5167.

FRAUNCES TAVERN MUSEUM. Directions: Located at 54 Pearl Street. Pearl Street crosses Wall Street. **Season:** Year round. **Admission:** Donation requested. **Telephone:** (212) 425-1778.

SOUTH STREET SEAPORT MUSEUM. Directions: The Museum Visitors' Center is located at 207 Water Street. **Season:** Year round. **Admission:** Charged, to restored ships and formal museum exhibits. **Telephone:** (212) 669-9400.

THE SOUTH STREET VENTURE. Directions: Located at 20 Front Street, in the center of the South Street Seaport. **Season:** Year round. **Admission:** Charged. **Telephone:** (212) 608-7888.

Midtown Manhattan

All paths on this plaza lead to Lincoln Center, the cultural capital of midtown Manhattan.

Midtown Manhattan is famous for glitter and glamour. A host of topnotch museums and theaters combine to create a cultural hotbed that's tough to beat, and the eclectic choice of shops, places to eat, and people to watch along the way adds a dimension all its own. How you decide to approach this goldmine of attractions depends entirely upon your personal tastes and temperament. The most basic rule, however, is not to let yourself be overwhelmed by the enormity of it all. This part of the city is laid out in a grid pattern and, with a good street map, you won't have any trouble finding your way from one point of interest to another. You may want to take in a Broadway show or an evening of opera or other music at Lincoln Center. If you are a confirmed shopper, you might want to spend your time checking out the elegant department stores and boutiques that cluster along and near Fifth Avenue. We can't tell you which shows to see (they change too often) or where to shop (there are just too many choices). What we *can* do, though, is mention a few of the activities and important institutions that make the midtown area unique. New York is a huge and vi-

brant city, and here in the heart of Manhattan the pace is particularly upbeat. We're off and running!

Midtown Manhattan is dominated by **Rockefeller Center,** the largest privately owned business and entertainment complex in the world. You'll enjoy walking through the Channel Gardens, extending west from Fifth Avenue. If you visit in the winter, there's something downright romantic about ice skating in the sunken plaza. In the summer you can enjoy an al fresco meal amid the skyscrapers at the **American Festival Café.** Breakfast, lunch, and dinner are served, as are Saturday and Sunday brunch. You can sip on a concoction called "Cool o' the Evening," composed of Barbados rum, a hint of lemon, and "a muddle of mint and sugar," while colorful state flags fly overhead on a warm evening. The menu runs the gamut from chile and fettuccine to steaks and chicken dishes. If you'd like a crow's-nest view of Rockefeller Center, take the elevator up to the **Observation Roof,** at the top of the RCA Building, which is part of the complex. From the 70th floor you'll have a clear view of the city stretching out below.

For an insider's perspective on the entertainment industry, take a backstage tour. There are lots of choices available. The **NBC Studio Tour,** also in the RCA Building, reveals the behind-the-scenes workings of a major radio and television studio. You'll visit the sets of shows like "Today," "NBC Nightly News," and "Saturday Night Live," and you'll stop by the control room of WNBC-AM Radio. You'll learn about the latest in video effects and technology, including the techniques used to cover a major sporting event. There's even an opportunity to see yourself on camera. This is not a static tour, but rather a chance to visit a working studio, so keep your eyes peeled. You might just see a familiar face at work.

Other opportunities to sneak a peek behind the scenes include **Take the Tour: Lincoln Center for the Performing Arts.** You'll spend an hour visiting the Metropolitan Opera House, Avery Fisher Hall, and The New York State Theater. You'll see the massive revolving stages, computerized lighting and sound equipment, and lavish sets used to enhance performances by the Metropolitan Opera Company, the New York City Ballet, the New York Philharmonic, and the New York City Opera. If you are a devoted opera buff and would prefer an in-depth look at the workings of the opera house alone, reserve a place on the **Backstage Tour: Met-**

Get a behind-the-scenes look at the Metropolitan Opera House, Avery Fisher Hall, and the New York State Theater.

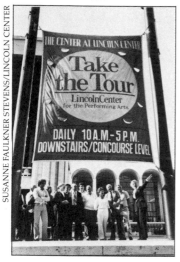

SUSANNE FAULKNER STEVENS/LINCOLN CENTER

ropolitan Opera House. You'll visit the workshops where craftsmen create the sets, costumes, and even the wigs used in the opulent productions. You'll visit rehearsal facilities and dressing rooms as well as the vast stage complex during the 1½-hour tour. You can also sign on for **Backstage at Radio City Music Hall,** an opportunity to explore the inner workings of the world-famous Art Deco palace where the Rockettes, as well as famous rock musicians, perform.

Theater tickets can cost a bundle in New York. If you want to go easy on your budget, check out the Theatre Development Fund's **TKTS Booth** at 47th Street and Broadway. Here you can buy day-of-performance tickets to a broad variety of Broadway and Off-Broadway shows for half price. Arrive early in the day and bring along something to read, as the lines are usually long. You might also want to drop by the **New York Convention and Visitors' Bureau** to see what "two-fers" are available. These coupons allow you to buy tickets at reduced prices, usually two-for-the-price-of-one, in advance or on the day of performance. They are usually issued for shows nearing the end of their runs.

New York is full of museums, including one that is truly unique. **The Museum of Broadcasting** collects and preserves radio and television programs, but, best of all, it also makes them accessible to the public. Only 11 years old, its collection includes 20,000 programs in cassette form, half TV and half radio, spanning more than six decades of broadcasting history. Here you can relive famous moments of your choice in comedy, drama, sports, and politics. Just head on up to the library, where a card catalog lists all the available programs. The selections are cross-referenced 25 different ways — by title, subject, date, network, and significant cast and production credits.

The museum admission fee entitles you to one hour of individually selected viewing/listening time. Choose the material that interests you, putting together 60 minutes' worth, fill out a request card for the librarian, then head for your assigned console in the Broadcast Study Center. There are 23 of these, and each can accommodate two people. Put on your earphones and relive man's first steps on the moon or the Beatles' first appearance on "The Ed Sullivan Show." Or spend your hour watching old political commercials or highlights from the Senate Watergate hearings. If you're a radio fan, you can renew your acquaintance with Jack Benny

Put on earphones and relive man's first steps on the moon or the Beatles' first appearance on the Ed Sullivan show.

or Fred Allen, or listen to some of FDR's early Fireside Chats.

The museum conducts more than six major exhibitions each year, and each one consists of 40 hours of programming. Films are shown on the 12-foot screen in the luxurious MB theater. Additional footage is aired in the two informal "Videotheques," each of which holds 40 visitors. Recent exhibitions have focused on Bob and Ray, Arturo Toscanini, and the Muppets. In addition, the museum has a collection of 2,400 rare radio production scripts with handwritten comments and corrections. Well over half of these have been transposed onto microfiche and are available to the public.

In the Museum of Modern Art's design collection, even the dinnerware and ashtrays are artworks.

Just a couple of blocks away, **The Museum of Modern Art** exhibits the finest works of modern art, from Post-Impressionism through the present day — paintings, sculpture, drawings, prints, architecture, photography, film, and industrial and graphic design are featured here. The list of noteworthy artists whose work is represented includes Pablo Picasso, Vincent van Gogh, Joan Miro, Henri Matisse, Roy Lichtenstein, Jackson Pollock, and Frank Stella. On the third floor, which is devoted to architecture and design, you'll see chairs, table lamps, dinnerware — even ashtrays — that prove themselves works of art in their own right. Films are shown daily in the two theaters on the lower level; you'll also find on this floor exhibits featuring items from the Museum of Modern Art Film Stills Archive. Weekday visitors may wish to take in one of the regularly scheduled Gallery Talks. Check the schedule in advance by telephone or when you enter the museum. The Garden Café is open for lunch, and for dinner as well on Thursdays. On a pleasant day you'll want to allow time to linger in the Abby Aldrich Rockefeller Sculpture Garden.

Our final suggestion takes you to a very different kind of institution. Devoted to the maintenance of international peace and security, **The United Nations** is an organization composed of more than 150 sovereign states. Each one has a voice in shaping a course of action designed to prevent international conflict and to promote, through international cooperation, the solution of economic, social, and humanitarian problems. Visitors are welcome at the U.N. Headquarters, located in midtown Manhattan on a site that is officially international territory.

Hour-long tours of U.N. Headquarters run seven days a week. As you walk through the complex, you'll hear people speaking many different languages and you'll pass delegates wearing saris and turbans. In keeping with the U.N.'s international character, guided tours are offered in 25 different languages. Your guide will explain the structure, aims, and activities of the U.N. He or she will also point out architectural features and artwork. The latter range from the Japanese Peace Bell, cast from coins and metals donated by citizens of 60 nations, to the teak statue of a woman with upraised arms, symbolizing mankind and hope, by Danish sculptor Henrik Starcke; from the Greek statue of Poseidon to *Single Form*, the huge bronze abstract work by English artist Barbara Hepworth, which is mounted in the circular pool in front of the Secretariat Building.

Your tour will take you through the Security Council Chamber, the Economic and Social Council, and other important parts of the U.N. You'll visit the cavernous blue, green, and gold General Assembly Hall, with its domed ceiling 75 feet high. The hall contains 2,000 seats to accommodate officers of the assembly, representatives of each member state, advisers, official guests, and the public. Each seat is equipped with earphones, which can be tuned to pick up either the voice of the speaker or a simultaneous interpretation in any of the U.N.'s six

The world meets in this room, and you can listen in when visiting the General Assembly Hall at the United Nations.

UN PHOTO 16544/MILTON GRANT

official languages: Arabic, Chinese, English, French, Russian, and Spanish.

The General Assembly is in regular session from mid-September to mid-December each year. Official meetings of the U.N. are open to the public; tickets are distributed free of charge at the Information Desk in the lobby of the General Assembly Building. Telephone ahead for details if you would like to attend a session.

You can tune each set of earphones to pick up the speaker's voice or a translation in any of six official languages.

Souvenir shopping at the U.N. is a little like visiting an international marketplace. You can purchase United Nations stamps at the United Nations Postal Counter (materials bearing United Nations stamps can only be mailed from U.N. Headquarters). The gift shop sells flags and handcrafts representing most of the member states. There is also a bookshop, where you can buy official U.N. publications, posters, and photographs. Greeting cards and stationery are sold at the UNICEF counter. Who would have imagined that a trip to midtown Manhattan would involve international travel?

ACCESS

ROCKEFELLER CENTER. Directions: The complex occupies the blocks between Fifth and Sixth avenues, 47th to 51st Street, with some buildings stretching even farther out. **Season:** Year round. **Admission:** Free. **Telephone:** (212) 489-2947.

OBSERVATION ROOF. Directions: Accessible by elevator from the lobby of the RCA Building, 30 Rockefeller Plaza. **Season:** Year round. **Admission:** Charged. **Telephone:** (212) 489-2947.

AMERICAN FESTIVAL CAFÉ. Directions: Located at Rockefeller Center. **Season:** Year round. Outdoor dining in warm weather. **Admission:** Free. **Telephone:** (212) 246-6699.

NBC STUDIO TOUR. Directions: Tours depart from the lobby of the RCA Building at 30 Rockefeller Plaza. **Season:** Year round. **Admission:** Charged. **Telephone:** (212) 664-4000.

TAKE THE TOUR: LINCOLN CENTER FOR THE PERFORMING ARTS. Directions: Tours originate on the concourse level, downstairs at Lincoln Center, at Broadway and West 64th Street. **Season:** Year round. **Admission:** Charged. **Telephone:** (212) 877-1800, ext. 512.

BACKSTAGE TOUR: METROPOLITAN OPERA HOUSE. Directions: Located at Lincoln Center. Tour assembly location will be provided when you make a reservation. **Season:** October through June. **Admission:**

Charged. **Telephone:** (212) 582-3512. **Note:** Advance reservations are required.

BACKSTAGE AT RADIO CITY MUSIC HALL. Directions: 1260 Sixth Avenue at 50th Street. **Season:** Year round. **Admission:** Charged. **Telephone:** (212) 757-3100.

TKTS BOOTH. Directions: Booth is located at 47th Street and Broadway. **Season:** Year round. **Admission:** Free. **Telephone:** (212) 247-5200.

NEW YORK CONVENTION AND VISITORS' BUREAU. Directions: Located at Two Columbus Circle (58th Street at Eighth Avenue). **Season:** Year round. **Admission:** Free. **Telephone:** (212) 397-8222.

THE MUSEUM OF BROADCASTING. Directions: Located at One East 53rd Street, just off Fifth Avenue. **Season:** Year round. **Admission:** Charged. **Telephone:** (212) 752-7684.

THE MUSEUM OF MODERN ART. Directions: Located at 11 West 53rd Street, between Fifth and Sixth Avenues. **Season:** Year round. **Admission:** Charged. **Telephone:** (212) 708-9400.

THE UNITED NATIONS. Directions: Entrance at First Avenue and 45th Street. Tours originate in main lobby. **Season:** Year round. **Admission:** Charged. **Telephone:** (212) 754-7713.

Tarrytown

SLEEPY HOLLOW RESTORATIONS

Tenant farmers brought grist for the mill to Philipsburg Manor, which fed New York City in the early 18th century.

For a taste of the early American good life, you can't do better than a trip to Tarrytown. Here you can visit a trio of meticulously restored, richly furnished mansions that tell the story of the settlement of the Hudson River Valley. Your day will be spiced with anecdotes that touch on literary tradition, the development of commerce, and early American political issues, as you explore the places where important figures of the 17th, 18th, and 19th centuries lived and worked. For variety's sake, you might want to add a trip to a Gothic Revival mansion. After all, it's in the neighborhood. And if you feel the need of a more modest influence, to balance all the opulence, we suggest a visit to a local church that dates back three centuries.

When Washington Irving called his elaborate romantic home "a little old-fashioned stone mansion, all made up of gable ends, and as full of angles and corners as an old cocked hat," he wasn't really all that far from reality. When he purchased **Sunnyside,** he didn't exactly become lord of the charming mansion you'll visit today. What he got for his money back in 1835 was an old Dutch farmhouse. What he ended up with, after extensive remodeling, was an ultraromantic home with lots of Gothic touches and a fanciful Victorian interior. He lived here comfortably with his nieces, enjoying the life of a well-to-do 19th-century gentleman.

The best part about Sunnyside is that it remains almost exactly as it was when Irving lived in it. You'll visit the study where he wrote his five-volume *Life of George Washington*, and you'll see the desk, presented to him by his publisher, G.P. Putnam, where he did much of his work. "Rip Van Winkle" and "The Legend of Sleepy Hollow" are only the tip of the Irving iceberg. In all, he penned enough manuscript to fill 20 volumes. The study is lined with shelves containing books that actually belonged to him.

Washington Irving described Sunnyside as "all made up of gable ends, and as full of angles and corners as an old cocked hat."

The parlor, decorated primarily in shades of pink, is furnished mostly in the Federal style. Here you'll see the author's own piano. His nieces Catherine and Sarah, who lived with him and served as his hostesses, used to accompany him on the flute. The charming dining room, where Irving continued to use only candles for illumination long after the rest of the house had been converted to oil, contains many original furnishings that represent his eclectic tastes. As you continue your tour, you get the feeling that this house belonged to a man who thoroughly enjoyed life. It is a comfortable, livable home — Irving called it his "snuggery" — where he indulged his own whimsical, fanciful nature.

Philipsburg Manor, Upper Mills was an early commercial site where Dutch settler Frederick Philipse constructed a shipping port and grist mill complex in the late 1600s. He shipped flour, cornmeal, and other commodities down the Hudson to New York City and from there to foreign ports. His business prospered, and he became one of the wealthiest men in the North American colonies, with vast landholdings here and elsewhere amounting to over 200 square miles. But his family came upon misfortune during the American Revolution. They sided with the British, and eventually all their holdings were confiscated by the Americans at the conclusion of the war.

Your visit begins with an orientation film shown in the comfortable theater. You'll learn that, in the first half of the 18th century, over a hundred tenant farmers brought their wheat here to Upper Mills to be ground into flour and shipped out. The manor became a vital commercial center, a "bread basket" for New York City and ports abroad. After the film, cross the wooden bridge over the pond and walk up the pathway paved with crushed oyster and clam shells (the Hudson used to be full of

Miller Charles Howell adjusts the flow of corn to the huge, turning millstones that grind the corn into meal.

shellfish) to the white stone manor house, with its whitewashed walls and scrubbed woodwork. There are no curtains in the windows and the floors are bare, a reminder that in the 18th century even a wealthy family lived a pretty Spartan life. Room contents include both Dutch pieces and furniture made in the Hudson River Valley.

Other buildings on the property include a 200-year-old barn where you'll meet Fresian Holsteins, black-and-white spotted cows similar to those that lived here in the time of Adolph Philipse, Frederick's son. The sheep in the sheepcote have long tails and horns, just like the sheep who lived here 200 years ago. From the barn, continue on to the mill, where you will find out how flour is ground. Geese swim in the millpond, weeping willows bow gracefully over the edge of the water, and the clock seems to have moved back to a quieter era. Take time to enjoy the serenity before returning to the main building, where there are some spiffy 20th-century interactive exhibits. You can push a button and hear the sounds of typical activities that would take place on the site at any given time of year. Women and children gather wheat and hay into sheaves in the fall. A fiddler plays while black slave women spin flax on a winter evening. Children squeal as they shove off on their sleds on a crisp winter day. . . .

Third of the Sleepy Hollow mansions, **Van Cortlandt Manor** has been restored to its appearance during the period 1750 to 1815. It sits prettily on a hillside overlooking the confluence of the Croton and Hudson rivers, just as it has for over two centuries. This was the home of the prominent Van Cortlandt family, whose members played important roles during the Colonial period and the Revolutionary War. You'll visit the old parlor on the ground floor, where rifles, powder horns, and a pair of antlers said to have been from a pet deer hang over the fireplace. In the nearby kitchen and milkroom, costumed staff members demonstrate domestic arts like cooking and medicine making. Your guide will lead you up a narrow staircase to the main floor with its more elegant parlor, furnished with pieces that range from Queen Anne-style to Chippendale to neoclassical. Up on the top floor you'll see the rooms where the family members slept.

The grounds are particularly varied and attractive, so allow time to stroll the "Long Walk," a brick path leading from the manor house to the old Albany Post Road and the Ferry House, where travelers stopped for food and lodging. You'll pass flower gardens, orchards, and a vegetable garden along the way. Just below the Ferry House, you can see the dock area where the ferry that traversed the Croton River used to tie up.

The next attraction is a little startling. Even though you know you've come to see a Gothic Revival mansion, you can't help but be amazed as you come upon a veritable castle sitting right on the edge of the Hudson River. **Lyndhurst** was designed by American architect Alexander Jackson Davis in 1838 as a residence for William Paulding, a former mayor of New York City who had also served as a general in the War of 1812. At the time, the Hudson River Valley was a center for romantic painting and architecture, and wealthy patrons of the arts commissioned elaborate residences like this.

The mansion is made from gray-white Sing-Sing marble. It has arched doorways and windows, vaulted ceilings, turrets, and even a tower, contributed by its second owner, George Merritt, a prosperous New York merchant who doubled the size of the already formidable edifice, raising the roofline and adding a new wing and a porte cochère. In 1880 the mansion was purchased by the wildly successful capitalist Jay Gould, who controlled Western Union Telegraph, the New York El, and the Erie Railroad. Gould used the mansion as a country retreat until his death in 1892, when the property passed on to his daughter Helen. Your tour guide will identify furnishings and mementos belonging to each of the families that contributed to the evolution of Lyndhurst.

You are welcome to walk the grounds here, to picnic, and to enjoy the rose garden, designed in a series of concentric circles. The floral display is at its height from the second week in June through mid-

No knight ever stormed its battlements, but Lyndhurst is still an honest-to-goodness castle on the banks of the Hudson River.

October. Just behind the garden, you'll see a vast greenhouse, desperately in need of repair. A greenhouse complete with Saracen tower was constructed by Merritt, but it burned the year Gould bought the property. This one was built in the Gothic style, and plans are underway to fund its restoration.

The Old Dutch Church of Sleepy Hollow, immortalized in Washington Irving's "The Legend of Sleepy Hollow," was built by Frederick Philipse as a place of worship for those who lived at his manor. Here is a church that has seen a lot in its time, some of it history and some of it fantasy. As you stand on the grassy rise that faces the stone building, imagine the early worshipers, arriving not by car but by horseback or perhaps on foot. If you take a walk in the adjoining graveyard, you'll see ancient gravestones with inscriptions carved in Dutch. A visit to the church helps to bring you back to reality. Life is, after all, more than just mansions.

Imagine early worshipers, arriving not by car but by horseback or perhaps on foot.

ACCESS

TARRYTOWN. Tarrytown is located on Route 9, just north of the Tappan Zee Bridge.

SUNNYSIDE. Directions: Located one mile south of the Tappan Zee Bridge on West Sunnyside Lane. Traveling north on Route 9, turn left at sign indicating way to mansion. **Season:** Year round. **Admission:** Charged. **Telephone:** (914) 631-8200.

PHILIPSBURG MANOR, UPPER MILLS. Directions: Located on Route 9, two miles north of the Tappan Zee Bridge. **Season:** Year round. **Admission:** Charged. **Telephone:** (914) 631-8200.

VAN CORTLANDT MANOR. Directions: Located in Croton-on-Hudson, nine miles north of the Tappan Zee Bridge. From Route 9, exit onto Croton Point Avenue. Continue one block east to South Riverside Avenue. Turn right and continue one quarter mile to entrance. **Season:** Year round. **Admission:** Charged. **Telephone:** (914) 631-8200.

LYNDHURST. Directions: Located on Route 9 in Tarrytown. **Season:** April through October, weekends only in November and December. **Admission:** Charged. **Telephone:** (914) 631-0046.

THE OLD DUTCH CHURCH OF SLEEPY HOLLOW. Directions: Located on Route 9 in North Tarrytown. **Season:** Weekends, June through August. **Admission:** Free. **Telephone:** (914) 631-1123.

For lodging and restaurant suggestions, contact the Sleepy Hollow Chamber of Commerce, 80 South Broadway, Tarrytown, N.Y. 10591. **Telephone:** (914) 631-1705.

Newburgh to Milton

Spend a day or two retracing General George Washington's famous footsteps along the banks of the Hudson River. The American Revolution takes on a human dimension that seldom seeps into textbook versions of the war, as you visit the places where the officers and enlisted men worked and lived, sometimes with their entire families along. This part of the state has continued its agricultural tradition, and it's fun to mix a visit to an orchard or a vineyard with stops at places important to American military history. What more pleasant way to pass an afternoon than picking apples and sampling wines? The general never had it so good.

Let's start in Newburgh, with its trio of military historic sites. At **Washington's Headquarters,** you'll begin your visit in the museum building, which contains an outstanding collection of Revolutionary War artifacts, all conveying a sense of what life was like for officers stationed here during the war. General George Washington and his staff used the adjacent Hasbrouck House for their headquarters from April 1782 until August 1783. Washington stayed here for 16 months, longer than at any of his other headquarters, and Martha Washington lived here too. It was here that he declared the war officially over in April of 1783. In 1850, the house and land became the first publicly owned historic site in the country.

The displays in the museum explain the strategic importance of the Newburgh area to the Continental Army. They also focus on the evolution of the American officer corps and the activities that took place at headquarters. It was here that officers threatened mutiny in what became known as the Newburgh Conspiracy. Washington managed to calm their anger, kindled because the government had not paid their wages, and avoid a major crisis. He had just been fitted with eyeglasses and won their sympathy when he began his address to them, saying, "Gentlemen, you will permit me to put on my spectacles, for I have not only grown gray, but almost blind in the service of my country."

You'll see the huge wooden booms and chains used to blockade British ships in the Hudson River at nearby West Point. Letters written at headquarters are among the original pieces displayed. There are also cannonballs the size of oranges, tin and

Washington won his officers' sympathy when he said, "Gentlemen, you will permit me to put on my spectacles, for I have not only grown gray, but almost blind in the service of my country."

Hasbrouck House in Newburgh was Washington's headquarters for 16 months and served as "a 1782 Pentagon."

leather waist-worn cartridge boxes, and French infantry muskets with bayonets. You'll discover that each officer of the Continental Army had to obtain his own uniform and that the quality varied according to each man's taste and wealth. One display focuses on insignia of rank — items like epaulettes, cockades, espontoons, and gorgets, the last being a holdover from medieval armor.

When you've finished at the museum, you can take a half-hour guided tour of Hasbrouck House, a Dutch fieldstone home overlooking the Hudson. It is arranged as it might have been in the 1780s, with period and reproduction furnishings. Our guide called the aides-de-camp room a "1782 Pentagon," because this is where the general and his men issued orders, took care of correspondence, and drew up important documents. Be sure to take a look at the field officers' beds, each one canopied and curtained to retain body heat.

Make your next stop **Knox Headquarters,** where General Horatio Gates, commander of the New Windsor Cantonment, made his headquarters during the winter of 1782–83. The stone Georgian house dates back to 1754, and it is furnished to represent the lifestyle of the family who lived in it then, the Ellisons. Museum staff members demonstrate 18th-century crafts, and outdoor concerts of period music are held in warm weather. Bring along a picnic and sit back and enjoy the setting.

Our favorite among this trio of related historic sites is the **New Windsor Cantonment,** where military life really comes alive, as costumed interpreters demonstrate typical tasks involved in 18th-century camp life. Start in the visitor center, where you can watch a 20-minute slide show that talks about the officers who died here and the tribulations involved in building the 800 log huts constructed with "regularity, convenience, and even some degree of elegance," in accordance with General Washington's orders. Take a look at the exhibits, like the one focusing on the "Badge of Military Merit," an award created by General Washington for enlisted men — the forerunner of the Purple Heart.

Follow the boardwalk through the woods to the campsite, where guides and exhibits interpret the last six months of the war. Before the huts were constructed, the cantonment was a veritable city of canvas shelters in many shapes and sizes. There were small white tents, eight feet long by six feet wide, which housed up to six men each. There were marquees and wall tents, tents to shelter horses and supplies, and even small bell tents designed to protect muskets from the elements. Remembering the difficulties and discomforts of their unfortunate colleagues at Valley Forge, the men constructed the log houses with dispatch.

Remembering the discomforts of their colleagues at Valley Forge, the men constructed the log houses with dispatch.

The cantonment accommodated 550 women and children as well as soldiers, and the day we visited one of the 20th-century women interpreters was hard at work making candles over an open fire. Another cooked up a batch of Indian fry bread while one man chopped wood and another molded musket balls in the fire. While the visitor center contains authentic 18th-century artifacts, the campsite is outfitted with reproduction pieces, so that visitors can handle them. That hank of tobacco you're holding was used as a room deodorizer and that lead pencil was used to write on a slate. Those odd metal lumps with the spots on them are gambling dice.

The cantonment also includes reproduction log houses (the original ones sold at auction for about a dollar apiece at the end of the war), including the Temple Meeting House, where 500 officers and their wives gathered to celebrate the alliance with

At Royal Kedem Winery, Ernest Herzog's well-trained nose tests the bouquet of a quality wine.

France. A blacksmith is usually at work in the blacksmith's shop, and each afternoon there's a demonstration of a military drill complete with musket or cannon firing. Plan to spend a couple of hours and by all means bring along a picnic.

For a change of pace, take a guided 1¼-hour tour of **Brotherhood Winery,** the oldest winery in the country. You'll wander through the cool underground cellars where wines mellow and age in huge wooden casks, just as they have for over a century. You'll learn the ins and outs of wine production, beginning with the selection and planting of the grapes, and you'll visit the processing and bottling area. A slide presentation introduces the seasonal activities involved in making wine, including the harvest season when the grapes are picked and crushed. And, naturally, each tour ends with a winetasting session, where you can sample the product. There is even a cheese shop, where you can put together a snack to enjoy with your newly purchased bottle of wine out in the picnic grove.

If you visit Newburgh in the summer or fall, you can enjoy a slight detour. Take time to drive up Route 9W from Newburgh to Milton, a particularly scenic stretch of road that's rich with orchards and wineries. At **Westervelt Clarke's Fruit Farm,** you can pick your own apples (September and October) and pears (September). During the picking season, kids will enjoy the tractor trailer rides out to the orchard. They'll also meet up with farm animals just waiting to have their ears scratched. At **Hepworth Farms Market,** you can stock up on fresh fruits and vegetables, including homegrown corn, plums, and peaches, as well as over 40 varieties of apples from their own orchards. Honey, jams, and cheeses are sold here too, along with fresh-baked apple pies and irresistible apple cider donuts. In the fall, you can watch cider being pressed in the mill. There are also several vineyards along this road. Best equipped for visitors is **Royal Kedem Winery,** which offers a tour of the winery, a film about winemaking, and a tasting in their 130-year-old converted railroad station. The people here can give you information on other area wineries that also offer tastings.

ACCESS

NEWBURGH. From I-87 (the Northway), take exit 17. Follow Route 17K west to Newburgh.

WASHINGTON'S HEADQUARTERS. Directions: From Route 17K in Newburgh follow signs to headquarters. **Season:** April through December. **Admission:** Free. **Telephone:** (914) 562-1195.

KNOX HEADQUARTERS. Directions: Headquarters are located about a mile from the New Windsor Cantonment, in Vails Gate. Follow Route 32 from the center of Newburgh to Forge Hill Road. Turn left and continue to entrance. **Season:** April through December. **Admission:** Free. **Telephone:** (914) 561-5498.

NEW WINDSOR CANTONMENT. Directions: From I-87 (the Northway), take Exit 17. Follow Route 300 one and a half miles to Temple Hill Road; turn left and continue another one and a half miles to entrance. From downtown Newburgh, take Route 32 to Vails Gate; turn right on Temple Hill Road and proceed one mile to entrance. **Season:** Mid-April through October. **Admission:** Free. **Telephone:** (914) 561-1765.

BROTHERHOOD WINERY. Directions: Follow I-84 west from Newburgh to Route 17. Turn left on Route 17 and continue south to Route 208. Turn left on Route 208 to Washingtonville and the winery. **Season:** Tours operate daily from May through October; weekends only February through April and November. **Admission:** Charged. **Telephone:** (914) 496-3661.

WESTERVELT CLARKE'S FRUIT FARM. Directions: Traveling north on Route 9W from Newburgh, turn left on Willow Tree Road in Milton, just after you pass the Ship Lantern Inn. Follow signs to farm. **Season:** June through October. **Admission:** Free. **Telephone:** (914) 795-2270.

HEPWORTH FARMS MARKET. Directions: Located on Route 9W in Milton. **Season:** June through December 1. **Admission:** Free. **Telephone:** (914) 795-2142.

ROYAL KEDEM WINERY. Directions: Located at Route 9W and Dock Road in Milton. **Season:** Year round; Sundays only from December through April. **Admission:** Free. **Telephone:** (914) 795-2240.

For lodging and restaurant suggestions, contact The Visitors' Center, Newburgh Preservation Society, 87 Liberty Street, Newburgh, N.Y. 12550. **Telephone:** (914) 565-6880.

Rhinebeck

In the late 1680s, a small group of Dutchmen purchased a tract of land along the Hudson River from a similarly small group of Indians. Nine years later, an Englishman, Judge Henry Beekman, obtained a land grant from the English Crown and settled himself nearby, on the site of the present village of Rhinebeck. In 1715, some 35 German families, fleeing religious persecution in the valley of the Rhine, came to the area as tenant farmers. Rhinebeck began to prosper, and soon became known as "The Breadbasket of New York City." Riverboats worked the Hudson north and south, transporting produce along with locally manufactured products like cooperage, leather goods, and clothing.

A thriving country town, contemporary Rhinebeck has not forgotten its Dutch, English, and German roots. Its name is believed to have originated with the German settlers, reminded by the Hudson of the beloved Rhine River they'd been forced to leave behind. The oldest church in town, the Dutch Reformed Church, with its lovely fanlight window and bell tower, was built in 1808 and still stands proudly on Mill Street. And Henry Beekman has been immortalized in the Beekman Arms Hotel, which claims to be the oldest hotel in America, dating back to 1766 (possibly sharing the honor with the Wayside Inn in South Sudbury, Massachusetts). Today there are fewer than 3,000 residents of Rhinebeck, and yet the center of town is a busy commercial district lined with attractive shops and restaurants. Outside of town, you'll travel through miles of gently rolling countryside, where farming is still a time-honored way of life.

Crowds of visitors flock to Rhinebeck late each August to visit the week-long annual **Dutchess County Fair.** This gala event includes horse shows, harness racing, stage performances, lots of music, and a large midway, along with demonstrations as varied as hypnotism and 4-H guide dog exercises. Livestock judging and ox pulls, rabbit showmanship and sheep shearing demonstrations are all part of the fun. You'll see the very best in produce, field crops, and arts and crafts, too.

The Beekman Arms Hotel dominates the center of Rhinebeck. At one time during the Revolutionary War, the entire population of the village

At one time during the Revolution, the entire population of Rhinebeck sought refuge within the inn's sturdy walls.

sought refuge within the inn's sturdy walls, after a minuteman brought word of a possible British attack. (Fortunately, the conflict never materialized.) During the years following the war, the inn served as a stagecoach stop on the New York City to Albany route, becoming a sort of town information center. Famous guests throughout the years included Washington, Lafayette, Horace Greeley, William Jennings Bryan, and Franklin D. Roosevelt, who had the habit of winding up each of his campaigns, whether for governor or president, with an informal talk delivered on the inn's porch.

Franklin D. Roosevelt used to wind up each of his campaigns with an informal talk on the inn's porch.

The Tap Room, with its low beams and paneled walls hung with treasured muskets, sabers, powder horns, maps, deeds, and other historical mementos, is a pleasant place to stop in for a drink. The inn is known for its hearty country fare, served in several dining rooms. The groaning board is laden with casseroles, salads, meats, breakfast foods, and even desserts at the buffet-style brunch served each Sunday. If you wish to spend the night, call well ahead to reserve one of the comfortable rooms with an old-fashioned flavor.

One favorite way to spend the evening in Rhinebeck is to take in a movie at **Upstate Films,** right in the downtown area. Film directors, critics, and producers sometimes offer special lectures. The schedule offers a mélange of foreign and Hollywood classics, independent features and new re-

Roll 'em! Moviegoers settle in for the feature film at Upstate Films in Rhinebeck.

leases, documentaries, animations, and the avant-garde. A typical one-week period might include *Tokyo Story* (Japan, 1953), *Giant* (U.S., 1950, starring Elizabeth Taylor and James Dean in his last role), *Jules and Jim* (France, 1961), and *Matter of the Heart* (U.S., 1985, a portrait of Carl Jung), the last accompanied by a lecture courtesy of a Jungian analyst.

At the **Old Rhinebeck Aerodrome,** you'll see aircraft dating back to 1900. There's the 1909 Bleriot XI, the first plane to cross the English Channel and also the first mass-produced aircraft. The wooden propeller and frame are set on what look like bicycle wheels. There's a copy of the 1911 American Curtiss "D," which daredevil Lincoln Beachey looped and plunged into the gorge at Niagara Falls. There's a British Tiger Moth, too, the same type used to train Royal Air Force pilots during the Second World War. Take a look at the 1942 red-and-yellow Canadian Fleet 16B; it still has a wooden propeller, but the frame is metal and the wheels are rubber. The 16B was used to train the pilots who later flew the famous Spitfire fighter planes.

If you visit the aerodrome on a weekend, you'll be able to do more than just admire old planes in their hangars. Air shows are held every Saturday and Sunday afternoon. Pilots show how the planes work and fly the oldest ones the length of the runway. Aircraft from the pioneer and Lindbergh eras show their stuff on some days. At other performances, Percy Goodfellow and The Black Baron perform, engaging in a mock dogfight and bombing raid in World War I aircraft. A tank and several cars of the same period maneuver on the ground below as the drama unfolds.

On weekends you can also put on some goggles and a tight white helmet and take a ride in a 1929 open cockpit biplane. You sit up front, with the pilot behind, engulfed by the roar of the engine. The pilot will take you on a 15-minute spin over the Hudson Valley, with views of the Catskills and the Kingston-Rhinecliff bridge, wrapping up with a flashy series of wing-overs, dives, and "waves," before settling on the grassy landing strip.

Driving around Rhinebeck, you'll see plenty of well-kept farms, but here's one that welcomes visitors each week from Wednesday through Saturday. If you like to work with yarn, you'll love **The Vane Sheep.** Here at Rhinecrest Farm, Phyllis and Dean Hunter raise sheep and sell sheep-related goods. There are usually Columbia and fine-wooled black sheep grazing peacefully in the pasture near the

Put on goggles and a tight white helmet and take an exhilarating ride in a 1929 open cockpit biplane.

World War I aviators trained on models like this Curtiss "Jenny" biplane, still flying at Old Rhinebeck Aerodrome.

classic red barn. Technically a shop devoted to fiber arts, The Vane Sheep also sells live lambs, fully dressed lambs (grain-fed and hormone-free) for your freezer, fleeces, electric fencing, and hay.

The shop itself is stuffed with baskets and shelves filled with wonderful yarns — wool, silk, cotton, linen, and alpaca — in dozens of different colors and textures. If you see a yarn you would like to use, a computer on the premises will spit out a custom pattern, coordinating the material with your style preference, size, and knitting gauge. Knitting, weaving, and spinning accessories and equipment are sold here too, including spinning wheels, knitting machines, and looms. And there are finished products to choose from — woolly sweaters, caps and mittens, socks and scarves, sheepskin slippers, and earmuffs.

The Vane Sheep sponsors an ongoing series of workshops and classes. Some of the subjects covered in these single-session workshops include introduction to knitting machines, net darning (a Victorian embroidery technique), country wreaths, introduction to floor looms, designing on the loom, and special needlepoint techniques. This is a comfortable, friendly place, where you'll enjoy improving old techniques or learning new ones in the air-conditioned/heated studio overlooking a pond and fields.

A few miles north of Rhinebeck, in Germantown, you can visit **Clermont,** home of Robert R.

A computer on the premises will spit out a custom pattern, coordinating the yarn with your style preference, size, and knitting gauge.

Livingston (1746–1813), and now the focal point of a 450-acre state historic site. Livingston was a famous chancellor of New York State. He shared the home with his mother, Margaret Beekman Livingston, a descendant of Judge Henry Beekman. The Chancellor's fascination with things mechanical drew him into a partnership with Robert Fulton, a relationship that culminated in the first successful steamship, *The North River Steamboat,* later renamed the *Clermont,* which paid its respects at the Chancellor's dock on its maiden voyage up the Hudson River in 1807.

Architecturally, the house has been restored to its 1930s appearance, but it is decorated in the Colonial Revival style, popular in the 1890s. It contains furniture used by seven generations of Livingstons. Originally built in 1730, the house was burned by the British during the Revolution and later rebuilt by heiress Margaret Beekman. So vast were the Livingston holdings that, when the lord of the manor looked out from the Dutch front door at a vista encompassing the Hudson and the Catskills beyond, he could rightfully say that he owned everything he saw.

Your tour guide will point out interesting portraits, including an original Gilbert Stuart of Margaret Beekman painted shortly before her death and an original Thomas Sully of Andrew Jackson, signed in the horse's bridle. The tall glass-fronted cabinets in the library contain nearly 3,000 volumes belonging to the Livingston family. There's even a complete set of Diderot's *Encyclopédie* in French.

When you leave the house, take a walk along the paths in the walled formal garden. If you want to have a picnic, you'll find tables and grills right along the banks of the Hudson River, adjacent to the parking area. Many special events are held at Clermont throughout the season, so be sure to write ahead for a calendar if you would like to plan your visit to coincide with the Clermont Open Croquet Tournament, the Independence Day Celebration, Hudson River Steamboat Days, the Pumpkin Painting Festival, or Christmas at Clermont.

ACCESS

RHINEBECK. Follow the Taconic Parkway to Route 199. Take Route 199 west to Route 308. Follow Route 308 into Rhinebeck.

DUTCHESS COUNTY FAIR. Directions: Held at the Dutchess County Fairgrounds in Rhinebeck. **Season:** One

Visit Clermont, perhaps the only mansion ever to have a steamboat named after it — and the very first steamboat at that!

week, at the end of August. **Admission:** Charged. **Telephone:** Call the Chamber of Commerce for information. **Note:** For information in advance of the fair, write Fairgrounds, P.O. Box 389, Rhinebeck, N.Y. 12572.

THE BEEKMAN ARMS HOTEL. Directions: Located on Route 9 in the center of Rhinebeck. **Season:** Year round. **Admission:** Free. **Telephone:** (914) 876-7077.

UPSTATE FILMS. Directions: Located at 26 Montgomery Street in downtown Rhinebeck. **Season:** Year round. **Admission:** Charged. **Telephone:** (914) 876-2515.

OLD RHINEBECK AERODROME. Directions: From the center of Rhinebeck, follow Route 9 north about 3 miles. Watch for sign, and turn right on Stone Church Road; continue following signs to aerodrome. **Season:** May 15 through October. Airshows and barnstorming rides on weekends only. **Admission:** Charged. **Telephone:** (914) 758-8610.

THE VANE SHEEP. Directions: Located on Route 9G just north of Rhinebeck. **Season:** Year round. **Admission:** Free. **Telephone:** (914) 876-2528.

CLERMONT. Directions: Follow Route 9G north from Rhinebeck to Route 6. Turn left on Route 6; travel west, following signs to Clermont State Historic Site, located in Germantown. **Season:** Mansion open Memorial Day through the last weekend in October. Historic site is open year round. **Admission:** Free. **Telephone:** (518) 537-4240.

For lodging and restaurant suggestions, contact the Chamber of Commerce, 22 East Market Street, P.O. Box 42, Rhinebeck, N.Y. 12572. **Telephone:** (914) 876-4778.

North Chatham to Catskill

O nly three hours' drive from Boston and two hours from New York City, nestled between the Catskill Mountains and the Berkshires, the area from North Chatham to the town of Catskill offers insight into several historical and cultural traditions. The Shakers, known for their inventions, their furniture, and their unusual lifestyle, formed a community in nearby New Lebanon, and their heritage is now preserved in a fine museum. Dutch and German farmers settled here in the 17th century, and their mark is still evident. And Hudson River School artist Frederic Church built his castle home in this part of the Hudson River Valley, overlooking the kind of vista that so influenced his work.

The Shaker Museum at Old Chatham is just 12 miles from Mt. Lebanon, where, in 1787, the Shakers established what was to become their first and most notable community. The museum is far out in the country, accessible by winding rural roads. It is difficult to believe what's in store as you begin your exploration of the quiet, charming complex of red farm buildings that make up the museum. Inside you'll discover the largest and most diversified collection of Shaker artifacts anywhere in the world. The exhibits are designed to showcase not only the objects, but also the processes by which they were made. You will see example upon example of fine Shaker chairs, but you'll also visit a cabinetmaker's shop and a chair factory. You'll see fine woolen cloaks lined with silk, a style patented by the Shakers around the turn of the century, and you'll see the looms that produced the fabrics and the cloak-cutting benches where the garments took shape.

You'll see the looms that produced the silk-lined cloaks and the cutting benches where they took shape.

The items on exhibit range from one of the earliest known Shaker pieces, a counter with the original reddish stain on top (made in Canterbury, New Hampshire, in 1792), to more commonplace drainage tubs and racks. You'll see fine cathead baskets, seed buckets, apple barrels, butter firkins, and containers for pickling and preserving meats. You'll also see fine cabinetry, like the enormous sorting and storage cabinet with four broad doors, chock-full of shelves and cubbyholes.

The main building has nine period rooms, a Shaker schoolroom, and shops that provide insight

The Luykas Van Alen House in Kinderhook is a reminder of New York's Dutch colonial days.

into the Shaker seed and medical industries. The Shakers were known for their conflicting tendencies toward withdrawal and involvement. Their religious habits and beliefs isolated them from the world at large, and yet they had to travel widely to market their various products; often they had to defend their pacifist stance and other beliefs to outsiders. The Shakers saw no separation between work and worship; for them, work done well was in itself a form of worship. They stressed simplicity in design and held that beauty derived not from external ornamentation, but from the "singleness of purpose brought to each piece."

The Dutch established farms in Kinderhook in the 1660s, and **The Luykas Van Alen House** has been preserved as a restoration museum of the Dutch Colonial period. Luykas built this house in 1737, and here he and his wife Elizabeth raised three sons. Today, the farm lays claim to only 30 of its original 500 acres. The house is one of the few surviving parapet-gable Dutch houses (the end walls extend above the roof), and the only one that has been restored to its early appearance. This type of architecture was commonplace in the Netherlands, and was used in the Hudson River Valley into

The mahogany staircase with its uncommonly low risers was built for Mrs. Church, who was uncommonly short.

The main staircase curves gracefully above the entrance hall in the Federal-style House of History.

the 1750s. You'll notice other typically Dutch features like the steep pitch of the roof, the brightly painted trim, and the arrangement of the living spaces.

Your guide will take you through the "first room," which was reserved for special occasions like baptisms and weddings, as well as being a place to receive guests. The kitchen was a sort of common room, used as an informal gathering place. It served other functions too, as is evident from the curtained bed in the corner. Walk through a connecting passageway to the third room, a more private area used as a family parlor or workspace. With spacious cellars and garrets, there was little need for the plethora of outbuildings common on so many farms. Workspace and storage space were built right into the house.

You'll notice typical Dutch touches like the Delft fireplace tiles brought from the Netherlands and the heavy Dutch Bibles, which speak of ties with the church left behind. Other furnishings were made right here in the Hudson River Valley, like the towering "kas" or linen cupboard and the scripture paintings. Bold lines and strong colors are evident throughout.

Also in Kinderhook, you can visit **The House of History,** a Federal-period house museum built around 1819. The house is characterized by high plastered ceilings and generously proportioned windows, melding Hudson Valley architectural tradition with a New England influence. It is filled with paintings, furnishings, and artifacts that reflect changing styles during the early decades of the 19th century. As you tour the rooms, you'll become acquainted with James Vanderpoel, the energetic attorney who lived in the house and who was active as a state assemblyman and later as a justice of the State Supreme Court. During the 19th century, Kinderhook sent more native sons to public office than any other small village in the country.

"About one hour this side of Albany is the center of the world. I own it," wrote Frederic Church. Take a 45-minute guided tour of **Olana,** the 19th-century Persian-style villa that Church, a prominent artist, built as his home. With its mosaic-patterned roof and façades, the villa presents a romantic image as you approach. Once inside, you will see an ambitious collection of imported furnishings and accessories, in addition to many original Church landscape paintings (inspired by the Hudson River, which winds past below the towering Victorian estate). There are Persian candle lanterns and oriental incense burners, Chinese import chairs and Turkish kalims. The architecture incorporates personal touches, like the mahogany staircase with its uncommonly low risers, which make for an unusually gradual pitch. That's because Mrs. Church was uncommonly short, and climbing regular stairs was wearing for her.

The fireplace in Church's study is decorated with tiles from Teheran; the Arabic stenciling on some of the walls picks up the colors in his paintings. You'll pass through the butler's pantry with its museum-quality collection of china and its wonderful double copper sink. It seems the family liked to use a different china pattern for each course, and the copper sinks meant less china chippage. Continue on into the combination dining room/picture gallery, which Church called his "one old room." It has a 17-foot ceiling, and the decor reflects the influence of medieval castles.

Be sure to allow time to walk the grounds of Olana. There's a fenced garden overflowing with well-tended blossoms, and there are also trails to explore. Bring along a picnic to spread out on this fine hilltop overlooking the Hudson. You'll feel like you're part of a painting yourself.

For a change of pace, try the **Catskill Game Farm.** Young children will love its old-fashioned carnival atmosphere. In the spring the farm overflows with young animals, and there are always fawns and baby goats to pet and feed. It's fun, too, to watch the bear cubs jumping into their feeding dishes and knocking each other off their balance beam. The farm is large, and you should expect to do lots of walking, although there is also a tractor train you can use to get around. Your young ones will probably want to spend a good portion of their time in the funky, nostalgic amusement area, riding the merry-go-round or taking a trip on a miniature Mercedes or motorcycle.

Whether you want to spend a few days camping or just need a few hours' break from sightseeing, **Lake Taghkanic State Park** is a pleasant respite. Facilities include two beaches, picnic areas, playgrounds, and a fitness trail. There are also rowboats to rent, if you would like to venture out onto the lake. Winter visitors enjoy ice skating, crosscountry skiing, and ice fishing. In the summer, the park offers a series of family-oriented activities, including nature hikes and crafts, square dances, puppet shows, films, and concerts.

From its mosaic roof to its oriental furnishings, artist Frederic Church built Olana as a celebration of the East.

Watch the bear cubs jump into their feeding dishes and knock each other off their balance beam.

In addition to tent sites, the park rents cabins and cottages, which come complete with beds or bunks and other basic furnishings, cookstove, refrigerator, electricity, and running water. Bring along your bedding, cooking equipment, and utensils. From late June to Labor Day, there is a two-week limit on campsite and cabin occupancy, with a one-week minimum stay. Off-season, the minimum stay is two nights. Be sure to write ahead for a reservation form.

ACCESS

Note: The towns and sites included in this trip are accessible from the Taconic Parkway.

THE SHAKER MUSEUM AT OLD CHATHAM. Directions: Take the Taconic Parkway to Exit B2. Go east on County Road 13 and then follow signs. Museum is located one and a half miles southwest of Old Chatham on Shaker Museum Road. Toll booth attendants often have printed directions on hand. **Season:** May 1 through October 31. **Admission:** Charged. **Telephone:** (518) 794-9100.

THE HOUSE OF HISTORY. Directions: Located 11 miles north of Hudson on Route 9 in Kinderhook. **Season:** Memorial Day through Labor Day. **Admission:** Charged. **Telephone:** (518) 758-9265.

THE LUYKAS VAN ALEN HOUSE. Directions: Located on Route 9H in Kinderhook. **Season:** Memorial Day through Labor Day. **Admission:** Charged. **Telephone:** (518) 758-9265.

OLANA STATE HISTORIC SITE. Directions: Follow Route 82 west from the Taconic Parkway to Route 23; continue on Route 23 to Route 9G in Hudson. Go south on Route 9G about 4 miles to Olana. **Season:** Memorial Day through Labor Day. **Admission:** Charged. **Telephone:** (518) 678-9595.

CATSKILL GAME FARM. Directions: From Hudson, travel west on Route 23 to Route 32. Turn left onto Route 32; travel south to sign for farm. Follow signs to the farm. **Season:** Mid-April through October. **Admission:** Charged. **Telephone:** (518) 678-9595.

LAKE TAGHKANIC STATE PARK. Directions: Follow the Taconic Parkway to Route 82. Go east on Route 82 to park entrance. **Season:** Year round. **Admission:** Charged. **Telephone:** (518) 851-3631. **Note:** For reservation form and information, write to the New York State Office of Parks, Recreation, and Historic Preservation, Taconic Region, Staatsburg, N.Y. 12580.

For lodging and restaurant suggestions, contact the Columbia County Chamber of Commerce, 527 Warren Street, Hudson, N.Y. 12534. **Telephone:** (518) 828-4417.

Saratoga Springs

A fashionable 19th-century spa, where the well heeled came to try their luck at the casino, refresh themselves in the mineral springs, and bet on their favorite hunk of horseflesh at the racetrack, Saratoga Springs today retains much of its earlier appeal. The roulette wheel doesn't spin here anymore, but you can still soak in the soothing waters or place a wager on your favorite thoroughbred. You can even bed down in one of the very same hotels that catered to the likes of Diamond Jim Brady and Lillian Russell.

This lively summer resort is at its glory from mid-June through Labor Day, peaking in August during the racing season. The sidewalks are lined with flowerbeds and outdoor cafés as well as lots of park benches where you can sit and admire the elegantly restored Victorian and Edwardian building façades. You can spend the day exploring two museums that document a continued tradition of wealth, or you can swim, picnic, and golf in the sprawling state park. When the stars come out, visit the oldest continuously running coffeehouse in America for a night of jazz or folk music or spend

On your marks, get set, go! Harness racing at Saratoga Raceway is a sport that's truly a breed apart.

the evening at a performing arts center that hosts world-famous rock stars, ballet companies, and symphony orchestras. Saratoga Springs offers all this and more.

Entering town, you can't help but recognize the importance of the elegant equine. There are diners decorated with racehorse statuary and motels with names like Triple Crown and Turf & Spa. Lean metal racehorses flank the flower-filled planters in the courtyard of the new City Center complex.

A good way to orient yourself is to start out with a visit to the **Museum of the Historical Society of Saratoga Springs,** housed in a former casino, right in the middle of pleasant Congress Park. Built in 1870 by John Morissey — champion prizefighter, state senator, and congressman — the Casino served as a busy gambling establishment right up until 1911, when a subsequent owner sold it to the city. Today it contains artifacts relating to the city's past, particularly to its hotels, springs, entertainments, and famous residents.

High society still thrives in Saratoga Springs, as evidenced by an exhibit of ball gowns and other items related to the parties thrown here annually since 1978 by Mr. and Mrs. Cornelius Vanderbilt Whitney. On the eve of the Whitney Stakes race at the Saratoga Thoroughbred track, the Whitneys host a lavish event in the Casino. The menu is always the same: steakburgers, fish and chips, chicken salad, omelets, and ice cream sundaes, all served from booths ("I like to keep it like a country fair," comments the hostess). The theme, however, is always different. The carousel party featured a hot pink and turquoise color scheme. For the 1984 Winter Olympics Gala, the hall was decorated with white-flocked pines, white impatiens, and white petunias. A skating rink was assembled and local skaters entertained. The Whitneys arrived in a horsedrawn sleigh. Not bad, for August.

After your museum visit, take a walk through the downtown area. Turn down tiny Phila Street and stop in at **Mrs. London's Bake Shop,** with its pink-and-green-flowered drapes and turn-of-the-century-style fixtures. You can purchase fresh pastries to go or settle down at one of the marble-topped tables for brunch or lunch. We couldn't resist Belgian waffles with fresh strawberries and whipped cream, but you might prefer Grandma London's cheese blintzes served with sour cream and preserves. Lunch choices lean toward quiche ("classic not cliché"), fresh soups, and uncommon

For the 1984 Winter Olympics Gala, the Whitneys arrived in a horsedrawn sleigh — not bad, for August.

sandwiches like smoked turkey club complete with bacon, lettuce, tomato, and avocado. A slice of chocolate mousse cake with sabayon sauce makes a nice finishing touch.

The **Lyrical Ballad Bookstore** is on the same street, just as it has been for the past 15 years. Housed in the old Saratoga National Bank building, this antiquarian bookstore stocks approximately 30,000 volumes. The rarest ones live in the safety of the walk-in vault. It's easy to lose oneself, wandering through the labyrinthine halls that connect the four rooms. There is something for everyone here, with tons of leatherbound sets just perfect for gifts and particularly strong sections on dance and thoroughbred racing.

Phila Street's most enduring claim to fame is **Café Lena,** the longest continuously running coffeehouse in the country. Folk fixtures like Arlo Guthrie started out here (and his brother Joady was scheduled to perform the day we dropped by). The musical fare includes folk, standard jazz, and bebop. In true coffeehouse tradition, you can sip on a variety of coffees and teas while enjoying the music. Owner Lena Spincer, who opened the café doors 25 years ago, also offers fresh pastries made upstairs. Locals rave about the *revini* — a sweet Greek nut cake. In addition to the evening concerts, plays and poetry readings are offered, along with afternoon children's concerts.

Now that you've gotten a feel for the town, climb into your car and head for the major attractions that lie on the outskirts. It wouldn't seem right to visit Saratoga Springs without paying your respects at the track. The oldest active thoroughbred racetrack in the country, dating back to 1864, the **Saratoga Racecourse** hosts 24 days of racing each August. Post time is 1:30 P.M. and there is racing daily except Tuesdays. Reserved grandstand seats go on sale at 7:30 every morning.

Breakfast at the racecourse is a Saratoga tradition and one that offers a particularly good way of showing children the action. Breakfast is served on the terrace overlooking the track early each morning during the racing season. Jockeys exercise their mounts and grooms cool them down in the fresh, early morning air, while you down your eggs and orange juice.

If you want to see horses in action but can't plan your visit for August, you can still see harness racing at the **Saratoga Raceway,** where standardbreds do their stuff almost all year round.

Get a glimpse of high society, past and present, at the Museum of the Historical Society of Saratoga Springs.

The National Museum of Racing is located near the thoroughbred track. Devoted to preserving articles associated with the origins and history of horse racing and the breeding of thoroughbred horses, the museum contains sculptures, paintings, trophies, and all sorts of memorabilia. Here you'll see the saddle and boots used by John Loftus on Man o' War. You'll see the bowls and urns and mammoth trophies and other artifacts associated with racing greats like Citation, Secretariat, and Exterminator. During the racing season, the museum screens movies from its own collection each day, showing yesterday's and today's thoroughbreds in action.

The museum also contains over 200 sets of American racing silks in just about every color combination you can imagine. There are bright pinks and oranges, soft blues and grays. Some of the silks incorporate symbols like circles, targets, stripes, and stars, while many rely on simple combinations of solid colors. Silks belong to the owner (and are worn by the jockey), and no two owners have exactly the same combination.

If horses aren't your thing, there's still plenty of reason to visit Saratoga Springs. A day is hardly enough time for exploring **Saratoga Spa State Park,** which boasts the only natural mineral baths in the United States east of the Rockies. The Spa runs two bathhouses and, when all facilities are in full operation, over 3,000 treatments can be performed in a single day. All of the baths are private (some are called semiprivate, but this just means that the dressing rooms and resting areas are separate from the tub, while in the private facilities you remain in the same room for dressing, bath, and resting). You can enjoy a mineral bath for the price of a movie, or you can spend the price of a good dinner and enjoy a "90-Minute Relaxer."

"As the bubbles burst, natural carbon dioxide penetrates the pores of your skin, stimulating the blood flow."

One brochure describes the latter experience in these terms: "Millions of tiny bubbles paint your body and begin their massaging action. As the bubbles burst, the natural carbon dioxide penetrates the pores of your skin, stimulating the blood flow." The bath is followed by a 20-minute professional massage, after which, "you are then left in your room to rest between hot sheets for half an hour."

The 2,000-acre park also offers the Peerless Swimming Pool Complex, with an Olympic-size pool, a diving pool, and a wading pool. The complex can accommodate up to 3,000 visitors at one time. The separate Victoria Pool is a combination swimming/diving pool. There are also tennis courts and two golf courses to enjoy, not to mention the many attractive picnic areas, some with play equipment, bridges, and even a geyser. There are lots of trails to walk, and joggers and bikers will find any number of routes to please themselves.

In the evening, take in a performance at the **Saratoga Performing Arts Center,** which is located in the park. The summer home of the New York City Ballet in July and the Philadelphia Orchestra during August, the center has an amphitheater that can seat 3,500 in the orchestra, 1,600 in the balcony, and 7,000 on the sloping lawn. Major recording artists and TV personalities also perform here regularly throughout the summer months.

Ballet, orchestral music, and the great outdoors make Saratoga Performing Arts Center an attraction that's tough to beat.

If you feel the need for a brief respite from the lively pace of Saratoga Springs, take a sidetrip out into the neighboring countryside and pay a visit to the **Saratoga National Historic Site.** It's hard to believe that this tranquil setting — rolling pastureland where cows graze peacefully in the meadows and deer appear frequently by the side of the road — was once the site of quite a different scenario. It was here, in the fall of 1777, that American and British troops engaged in a pair of battles that forced the surrender of British General John Burgoyne and turned the tide in our country's fight for liberty. Although it would take the Colonial army four more years to achieve final victory at Yorktown, the battles of Saratoga were crucial because they occurred at a time when the Americans had begun to think their cause a hopeless one. The victory restored American resolve and induced a reluctant France to openly assist the colonists in their quest for liberty.

A visit to the Saratoga National Historic Site is a relaxed, low-key event, just perfect for history buffs. It's also a bargain, as there are no admission charges. You'll begin with a stop at the Visitor Center, where you will see a 21-minute slide show in the comfortable theater. By integrating contemporary views of the Hudson River with slides depicting 18th-century documents and battle scenes (ingeniously re-created with hundreds of toy soldiers), the show provides a lively orientation. The narrator explains that mastery of the Hudson River, a vital link in the transportation network, meant "defeat or victory, subjugation or freedom." Reading from the journal of one William McArthur, a Revolutionary-era farmer and wheelwright, the voice observes that the coming of the soldiers "robbed us of our

Camp life is serious business for latter-day American and British soldiers at Saratoga National Historic Site.

peace, our comfort . . . swept us up in tension and conflict."

After the slide show, take a look at the formal exhibits housed here, in which American Revolutionary artifacts — clay pipe, powder horn, cartridge box, prayer book, and the like — are displayed. There are also several dioramas, which illustrate the quick construction of embankments and redoubts. Pushbuttons activate narration. You can almost feel the crispness in the air shortly before the British surrender as a voice reads from *Campfires of the Revolution:* "The evening was setting in, gray and dusk; and as the nights of October are chilly in that high region, the campfires were blazing in the woods."

There's something heady about pacing the same ground where Burgoyne planned his strategy more than 200 years ago.

After exploring the center, head out to your car for a self-guided tour of the battlefields and related points of interest. (You will be given an annotated map to take along.) The complete tour is nine miles long and includes 10 stops. The road is one-way, so you can't change your mind and turn back, but you can always skip stops if you are in a hurry. There are plenty of parking areas where you can leave your car while you get out to explore and read the explanatory plaques, which offer just enough information so that you will find yourself re-creating the past in your mind's eye. Lines of stakes outline the position of important "redoubts" (systems of fortifications), further feeding the imagination.

Stops along the route include the Neilson Farm (Bemis Heights), where patriot farmer John Neilson's farmhouse still stands, looking much the same as it did in September 1777, when American staff officers used it for their headquarters. You'll peer out over the Barber Wheatfield, where 1,500 advancing British and German soldiers were intercepted by the Americans, forcing Burgoyne's troops to withdraw. You can walk down a path to the spot where Burgoyne had his headquarters (housed in a tent). There's something heady about pacing the same patch of ground where this famous general planned his strategy over 200 years ago.

Confirmed history buffs may want to proceed on to Schuylerville, eight miles down the road, to take a guided tour of **The Schuyler House,** the country home of General Philip Schuyler, who preceded Gates as commander of American troops in the Northern Department. During the 1760s the estate served as a busy center for farming, milling, and merchandising activities. Products were transported by Schuyler's own river fleet to places as far away as the West Indies.

The existing two-story house was said to have been built in less than a month, 17 days by some accounts. The walls were made of unburned brick nogging (sun-dried bricks) and the planks were hewn from lumber stored at a sawmill on the property (somehow overlooked by the British). The house is furnished with period pieces, as well as a few Schuyler family belongings, like the handsome linen chest. Some original straw flooring remains intact, and original wallpaper still hangs in the parlor where General Schuyler entertained prominent figures of his day, among them George Washington, Benjamin Franklin, and the Marquis de Lafayette. "My hobby horse," the general once wrote, "has long been a country life; I dismounted once with reluctance, and now saddle him again with a very considerable share of satisfaction, and hope to canter him on to the end of the journey of life."

The original wallpaper still hangs in the parlor where General Schuyler entertained Washington and Lafayette.

ACCESS

SARATOGA SPRINGS. Follow I-87 north to Exit 13. Take Route 9 north into Saratoga Springs.

MUSEUM OF THE HISTORICAL SOCIETY OF SARATOGA SPRINGS. Directions: The museum is located in Congress Park in the center of the city. **Season:** June through October, daily. Wednesday through Sunday afternoons only from the beginning of November until Memorial Day weekend. **Admission:** Charged. **Telephone:** (518) 584-6920.

MRS. LONDON'S BAKE SHOP. Directions: Located at 33 Phila Street. **Season:** Year round. **Admission:** Free. **Telephone:** (518) 584-6633.

LYRICAL BALLAD BOOKSTORE. Directions: Located at 7 Phila Street. **Season:** Year round. **Admission:** Free. **Telephone:** (518) 584-8779.

CAFÉ LENA. Directions: Located at 45 Phila Street. **Season:** Year round. **Admission:** Charged. **Telephone:** (518) 584-9789.

SARATOGA RACECOURSE. Directions: Traveling north on Broadway, the main street in Saratoga Springs, turn right on Circular Street. Then turn right on Union Avenue and continue to racecourse, on your right. **Season:** August. **Admission:** Charged. **Telephone:** (518) 584-6200.

SARATOGA RACEWAY. Directions: From Broadway, turn right on Lake Avenue. Then turn right on Nelson Avenue, and continue to track on your left. **Season:** January through March; May through November. **Admission:** Charged. **Telephone:** (518) 584-2110.

THE NATIONAL MUSEUM OF RACING. Directions: The museum is located across the street from the entrance to the Saratoga Racecourse. **Season:** Year round. **Admission:** Free. **Telephone:** (518) 584-0400.

SARATOGA SPA STATE PARK. Directions: The park is located south of the city, with entrances on both routes 9 and 50. **Season:** Year round, including baths. Pool complex is open late June to Labor Day. **Admission:** Charged. **Telephone:** For information on park facilities, (518) 584-2000. To make an appointment for mineral baths, (518) 584-2011.

SARATOGA PERFORMING ARTS CENTER. Directions: Located within Saratoga Spa State Park. **Season:** June through Labor Day. **Admission:** Charged. **Telephone:** (518) 587-3330.

SARATOGA NATIONAL HISTORIC SITE. Directions: Follow I-90 (New York State Thruway) to Rensselaer. Take Route 32 north approximately 30 miles to the entrance to the historic site. **Season:** Visitor Center is open year round, except for Thanksgiving, Christmas, and January 1. Road tour is open April 1 through November 30, weather permitting. **Admission:** Free. **Telephone:** (518) 584-2000.

THE SCHUYLER HOUSE. Directions: Follow signs to Route 4 as you exit Visitor Center parking lot. Turn left on Route 4 and travel north eight miles to Schuylerville. The house is located to the right off Route 4, just before you enter town. **Season:** Mid-June through Labor Day. **Admission:** Free. **Telephone:** (518) 584-2000.

For lodging and restaurant suggestions in the Saratoga Springs area, write to the Greater Saratoga Chamber of Commerce at 494 Broadway, Saratoga Springs, N.Y. 12866. **Telephone:** (518) 584-3255.

Ticonderoga to Plattsburgh

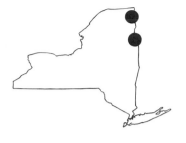

Snuggled up tight against the western border of Vermont, the Ticonderoga-to-Plattsburgh route combines a slice of history with a chance to experience America's oldest organized tourist attraction. This is a good trip for wanderers, people who like to explore a little here and a little there. There's a lot to do, but the activities are a bit spread out. Getting from one place to another is pleasant in itself, as you drive down country roads sprinkled with creatively spelled signs advertising shiners and crawfish. You'll get a strong sense of New York's proximity to Canada as you check out brochures written in two languages (J'aime New York) and listen to Canadian visitors speak French.

It was the French, in fact, who began construction of **Fort Ticonderoga,** which they called Fort Carillon, in 1755. Because of its location, perched on a rocky promontory overlooking both Lake Champlain and an outlet of Lake George, whoever controlled the fort also controlled travel between Canada and the American colonies. The fort has been nicknamed "Key to a Continent," an apt description in view of its vantage point and its history. Between

Everyone wanted the lakeshore view! Fort Ticonderoga was one of the hottest pieces of property in 18th-century America.

TICONDEROGA AREA CHAMBER OF COMMERCE

Between 1755 and 1777, Fort Ticonderoga was attacked six times. Three times it was held and three times it fell.

1755 and 1777, it was attacked six times. Three times it was successfully held and three times it fell, with the "key" changing pockets — a record no other fort on the continent can approach.

Enter through the sally port. A series of plaques forms a timeline tracing control of the fort from its early construction by the Marquis de Vauetreiul, Governor of Canada, to its subsequent takeover by the British in 1759. The fort fell again to Ethan Allen and the Green Mountain Boys in 1775, before control was re-established by the British in 1777. Ticonderoga is four sided, with pointed spurs or bastions extending from each corner. One bastion contained the cistern, which is still in use today. Another, complete with vaulted ceiling, housed the bakery. The southeastern bastion held the powder magazine, with stables built above, and the southwestern one was used for general storage.

As you explore the grounds, be sure to notice the row of 18th-century bronze cannon overlooking the lake. Some have wonderful carvings, like handles in the shape of serpents. The fort was first built to serve as a garrison for 400 soldiers. In times of war, though, thousands of men lived just outside the walls, housed in endless rows of tents.

Now pass on through the arched drive entering the Place d'Armes or Parade Ground (depending on who was in control), as you follow in the footsteps of famous figures like George Washington, Benjamin Franklin, Ethan Allen, the Marquis de Montcalm, Henry Knox, and Benedict Arnold. Peek into the musty jail cells. Take a look at an officer's bedroom, relatively luxurious with its bearskin rug, woven bed coverlet, and candlestand. The barracks houses the fort's museum, which includes some unusual pieces like the officers' mess table. Fourteen men sat on each side, and each person's place setting was stored in an individual drawer below his place. The museum also contains a potpourri of period artifacts: a lock of George Washington's hair, a rum horn given to General Schuyler by Paul Revere, Ethan Allen's pocket compass. . . .

You can wander through the fort independently or join one of the guided tours offered regularly throughout the day. Fife and drum music is performed on the Parade Ground at regular intervals by a dozen young musicians dressed in black tricorn hats, knee-length red coats, white breeches, and buckled shoes. A cannon shoot is also held several times a day. A target in the shape of a soldier awaits its fate out in the field beyond the fort walls. Watch

The more things change, the more they stay the same. The Fort Ticonderoga Ferry 110 years ago (top) and today (bottom).

as a costumed soldier moves the muzzle stop from the field cannon, retrieves the charge of black powder, pours the charge into the breech of the gun, follows this with a wad of grass for "ramming," and then with a ball. "If you hear no sound and see no mound, you know that ball is Vermont bound," he admonishes, before firing. With the smell of gunpowder in the air, the ball bounces awkwardly across the field, a few yards from the target. Such cannon, we learn, had a fairly long range but were difficult to aim accurately.

There is a large souvenir shop where you can purchase items like an Adirondack animal track chart or a reproduction British Army recruiting poster. There's a cafeteria here, too, serving breakfast, lunch, and snacks.

From the fort, it's only a couple of minutes' drive down a quiet country road to the **Fort Ticonderoga Ferry.** The road ends at a parking lot/landing, which gets a pleasant breeze off the lake on a hot summer day. There's a public boat ramp here, and you can usually see a few people fishing from the bank of the lake. A hand-lettered sign advises that this is the departure point for the ferry to Vermont and that Rutland is 38 miles distant, White River Junction 81 miles. Another sign says, "Continuous crossings — we'll be right back." We peer across the lake and see the ferry just starting to head out from the Vermont shore. She arrives a few minutes later, unloads seven cars, and starts loading passengers bound for the Green Mountain State.

The air smells of gunpowder as the cannonball bounces across the field, a few yards from the target.

There is something so simple about the whole process that it doesn't seem in sync with the 20th century. No lines, no reservations. Just good basic transportation when you want it.

Back in Ticonderoga Village, pay a visit to **Mount Defiance,** called Rattlesnake Mountain by the French (Serpent à Sonnette). The Americans called it Sugar Loaf Hill, and believed it couldn't be scaled. British General John Burgoyne thought otherwise and proved himself right, observing, "Where a goat can go a man can go, and where a man can go he can drag a gun." He successfully fortified the hill, changed its name to Mount Defiance, and from there eventually forced the Americans to flee from Fort Ticonderoga. Today a steep, narrow, paved road leads to the top of Mount Defiance. There are a couple of cannon at the top, but the real draw is the view, particularly spectacular in the fall.

The **Mount Hope Battery,** built by American troops and later occupied by Burgoyne's men, guarded communication between Lake George and Lake Champlain. Here you can explore several rustic, reconstructed buildings. In the sentry house, you'll see domestic artifacts found in the area, like a framed swatch of a Colonial quilt. Be careful not to stumble on the rough stone floor in the blockhouse as you examine the lookout holes and the niches for musket barrels worked into the thick wooden walls. You'll also see the remains of a Colonial-era gunboat, raised from Lake Champlain in 1953 with 408 cannonballs aboard.

Back in the village, you can get a feel for a more contemporary aspect of Ticonderoga's history by stopping at the tiny **Heritage Museum.** The exhibits here fall into basically two types. First, there are all sorts of items related to the battleship, U.S.S. *Ticonderoga,* which was commissioned in 1944 and which served as the primary recovery ship during the Apollo space flights of the early 1970s. Artifacts run the gamut, from a fragment of a Japanese kamikaze plane found embedded in the flight deck to a photo showing the *Ticonderoga* with the Apollo 17 command module floating beside it in the foreground.

Ever wonder how they get the lead inside pencils? The second group of items are those related to Ticonderoga pencils, the familiar yellow ones made by the American Graphite Company right here in Ticonderoga. The displays show how the pencils are made from a cedar slat. The slat is grooved, the leads glued in, and another slat is glued on top (like

As General Burgoyne observed, "Where a goat can go a man can go, and where a man can go he can drag a gun."

RICHARD K. DEAN

The river runs swift and deep, as your dory shoots through the heart of Ausable Chasm.

a two-part mold). Then the would-be pencils are cut and shaped, finished and packaged.

Now head north to **Ausable Chasm,** which has been operated as a public attraction since 1870. The chasm is a huge cleft with towering sandstone cliffs formed about five million years ago, when this part of the country was submerged beneath a prehistoric sea. The Ausable River flows through the chasm, winding 59 miles south from its headwaters at Mount Marcy to Lake Champlain. Through the years, the river carved deeper and deeper into a fault in the bedrock, sculpting the dramatic gorge. Major John Howe, who discovered the chasm, made his descent suspended on ropes. Today's visitors travel by foot, following stone steps up and down, and crossing steel bridges that span the gorge high above the river.

You'll buy your ticket in one of the hugest, gaudiest gift shops we've ever come across — souvenir kitsch heaven. There's also a cafeteria with a reasonably priced breakfast, lunch, and snacks. The Ausable Chasm complex also includes a miniature golf course, an arcade full of coin-operated games, a glassblower's shop where you can watch the artisan at work, a T-shirt store, and a campground.

Major John Howe made his descent suspended on ropes. Today's visitors follow the less hazardous stone steps.

The walk through the chasm is about three-quarters of a mile long and includes about 150 steps. The footing can be difficult, particularly if it has rained recently. Hike at your own pace, pausing where you like to take a break, enjoy the scenery, and read the explanatory signs. Pine trees form a canopy over the walkway in some places, while in other spots you'll find yourself shouldering up against towering rocks, damp with moss and ferns. Some trees appear to grow directly out of the rocky ledges. The walk takes about half an hour, and you'll end up at Table Rock, a platform extending over the river. From here on out, you'll travel by boat.

Some trees appear to grow straight out of the rocky ledges.

While you can hike at your own speed, be prepared for a wait when you get to Table Rock. On crowded days it can take half an hour on line before your turn comes to step into one of the oversized red wooden dories. (Each boat holds about 18 passengers.) For protection against the foamy waters ahead, you pull up the green plastic flaps attached to the sides. There are two guides on each boat, one in the prow and one in the stern. Boats like these have been carrying tourists through the chasm since 1900. Each one weighs about a ton, and they're all pulled back upstream on cables. You'll pass through the "Grand Flume," a stretch of river only 12 feet wide but 60 feet deep. The highlight of the 10-minute journey is a bouncing ride through a frothy set of rapids into the Whirlpool Basin. Let us stress that, while this is exciting, you need no prior experience to enjoy it. There were both young children and octogenarians in our boat and everyone enjoyed the trip. The hike is actually more of a challenge. When the boat ride is over, a bus takes you back to the main souvenir shop, where you started out.

For quite a different kind of boat trip, continue 12 miles north to Plattsburgh. Here you can take a sightseeing excursion aboard the **MV *Juniper*,** Lake Champlain's only excursion vessel. The ship holds up to 110 passengers and makes an 18-mile figure eight up the lake. During the two-hour cruise, you'll enjoy a lively narration delivered by Captain Frank Pabst, who has spent 30 years diving here in Lake Champlain and who ran a scuba diving business that was instrumental in the documentation and recovery of many historic artifacts, like the two 18th-century cannons he discovered. The captain also hosts a 4½-hour sunset cruise, or, if you're a real night owl, you can end your trip with the late-night cruise, featuring music for dancing under the stars.

ACCESS

TICONDEROGA TO PLATTSBURGH. All points on this trip are easily accessible from I-87 (the Northway). Take Exit 28 and follow Route 74 east to Ticonderoga. To reach Plattsburgh, continue north on Route 87, following signs to Plattsburgh. Coming from Vermont, you may wish to take the Fort Ticonderoga Ferry across Lake Champlain (see listing below).

FORT TICONDEROGA. Directions: Follow Route 74 east to the junction with Route 22. Follow signs to fort. **Season:** Mid-May through late October. **Admission:** Charged. **Telephone:** (518) 585-2821. **Note:** Price of admission also covers a visit to the **Mount Hope Battery,** reached by following Route 8 west into Ticonderoga. Turn right on Elk Drive and then follow signs ¾ mile to battery.

FORT TICONDEROGA FERRY. Directions: Follow Route 74 east, beyond entrance to fort, to ferry dock on bank of Lake Champlain. Ferry crosses to Shoreham, Vermont, and Route 74. **Season:** May 1 through last Sunday in October. **Admission:** Charged. **Telephone:** (802) 897-7999.

MOUNT DEFIANCE. Directions: From the center of Ticonderoga, traveling west on Route 8 (Montcalm Street), turn left on Champlain Avenue at traffic light. Bear left on The Portage, then left on Mount Defiance Street. Continue to tollbooth. **Season:** Mid-May through Columbus Day. **Admission:** Road toll charged. **Telephone:** None.

MOUNT HOPE BATTERY. For directions and season see Access entry for Fort Ticonderoga above.

HERITAGE MUSEUM. Directions: Located on Route 8 (Montcalm Street) in Ticonderoga. **Season:** July and August. **Admission:** Free. **Telephone:** None.

AUSABLE CHASM. Directions: From I-87 (the Northway), take Exit 34. Follow Route 9 to Ausable Chasm, 12 miles south of Plattsburgh. **Season:** Mid-May to early October. **Admission:** Charged. **Telephone:** (518) 834-7454.

M/V JUNIPER. Directions: Located at the foot of Dock Street, just past the railroad station, in Plattsburgh. **Season:** May 1 through September 30. **Admission:** Charged. **Telephone:** (518) 561-8970.

For lodging and restaurant suggestions, contact either the Chamber of Commerce, Montcalm Street, Box 70, Ticonderoga, N.Y. 12883 (**Telephone:** (518) 585-6619), or the Chamber of Commerce, 135 Margaret Street, P.O. Box 310, Plattsburgh, N.Y. 12901 (**Telephone:** (518) 563-1000).

The M/V Juniper *cruises Lake Champlain under two ensigns: the Stars and Stripes and the Maple Leaf.*

COURTESY CAPTAIN FRANK PABST

Lake Placid

Long known as the "Winter Sports Capital of the World," Lake Placid originally served as the site of the 1932 Winter Olympics. Modernized in 1980 to host another Olympic Games, this Adirondack resort village today is the home of the United States Olympic Training Center. Top athletes visit year round to train and compete. The Olympic Authority, established by the state of New York in 1981, manages specialized facilities that include the Mt. Van Hoevenberg Recreation Area, the Ski Jump Complex, the Speed Skating Oval, the Whiteface Mountain Ski Area, and the Whiteface Mountain Veterans Memorial Highway. Visitors are welcome at all of these sites.

Since Lake Placid is synonymous with the Olympics, begin your visit with a tour of some of the famous facilities. The **Mt. Van Hoevenberg Recreation Area** is the site of the only bobsled run in the United States. Sixteen hundred meters long, with a drop of 162 feet, it's the fastest run in the world. With 16 curves, including notorious Shady Corner (a 170-degree change in direction), the deep concrete trough twists down the mountainside like a huge snake. Bobsleds, manned by two- or four-man teams, can reach speeds up to 90 mph in competitive events.

Mt. Van Hoevenberg also has a luge run. The slider lies on his back on the narrow sled, his head raised just enough to see. The sled has no mechanical steering or braking devices. The slider controls its passage through the icy trench (which has much tighter curves than the bobsled run) with his feet and by shifting his weight.

Experience the "champagne of thrills" firsthand, as a professional driver takes you down the Olympic bobsled run.

If you visit in the off-season, you can walk around the bobsled and luge runs and take a truck ride up to the top of the mountain for a different perspective. In the finish-line building you can look at sleds and other equipment up close and watch videotapes of winter competitions, including some that ended in death. If you come during the winter, though, you can watch athletes training and racing almost every day. Passenger rides with professional drivers are available most weekends, should you wish to experience bobsledding, the "champagne of thrills," firsthand.

You can also take advantage of the 50-kilometer network of cross-country ski trails constructed

The bobsled run at Mt. Van Hoevenberg is the fastest in the world, with drivers barreling through at 90 mph.

for the 1980 Winter Olympics. Mt. Van Hoevenberg receives over 100 inches of snow annually, and there is almost always good skiing from early December to late March. The ski area is adjacent to the bobsled and luge runs. There's a warming lodge with waxing rooms, a ski shop, and a small snack bar. The complex includes 10 marked loops, providing three novice, six intermediate, and one expert tour, with additional expert opportunities located nearby.

The recreation area is also the setting for two first-class hunter/jumper horse shows, in the last week of June and the first week of July each summer. Top riders, including past and future members of the United States Equestrian Team, compete in the Lake Placid Horse Show and the I Love New York Horse Show. Events run all day long and refreshments are served cafeteria-style in a tent. In addition to regular snack bar fare, there are barbecued spareribs and homemade cakes.

Ski jumping is no longer just a winter sport, as you'll discover when you visit the **Olympic Ski Jump Complex.** Plastic matting replaces snow on the jumps during the warmer months, while athletes continue to train and compete. Step into the

"Great things are done when men and mountains meet." A lone hiker in the Adirondacks.

On a clear day, the view encompasses both the Montreal skyline and Vermont's Green Mountains.

glass-enclosed elevator and head up the equivalent of 26 stories to the top of the 90-meter tower. The view of the Adirondacks is terrific!

The Olympic Authority offers a package plan featuring reduced-price admission to Mt. Van Hoevenberg, the Olympic Ski Jump Complex, and two other attractions: **Whiteface Mountain Veterans Memorial Highway** and **Whiteface Mountain Chairlift.** The package is a bargain if you really plan to visit all four attractions, but you'll need more than one day to do that. If your time is limited, you're better off buying individual admissions.

Fifth highest of the state's mountain peaks, Whiteface Mountain is the only one of the 46 Adirondack High Peaks accessible by car. **Whiteface Mountain Veterans Memorial Highway** climbs up an eight-mile stretch, terminating just 500 feet short of the summit. You'll begin your journey by passing through an alpine-style gatehouse overlooking a lake at the base of the toll road. There are lots of scenic parking pull-offs where you can pause to enjoy the views on the way up. There's also a stone castle near the main parking area at the top, which houses a cafeteria and gift shop. To reach the summit, you can either climb up a stone stairway or take an elevator ride.

Still another way to get to the top of the mountain is to follow the short nature trail that originates behind the castle. Match the numbered markers with the information in your brochure (available at the base of the trail), and you'll learn how ice has shaped the mountain. You'll also become acquainted with alpine plants like the bearberry willow and the three-toothed cinquefoil. On a clear day, the panorama encompasses the Montreal skyline, Lake Champlain, Vermont's Green Mountains, and hundreds of Adirondack peaks and lakes.

You might choose instead to take a ride on the **Whiteface Mountain Chairlift.** You'll travel high above the Olympic racing trails on a two-stage trip that involves switching lifts at the mid-station lodge. Eventually you'll reach the peak of Little Whiteface. Be sure to allow about two hours for the round trip.

For a different kind of sightseeing, take time out to visit the **John Brown Farm,** the home and gravesite of abolitionist John Brown, immortalized in the song "John Brown's body lies a-mouldering in the grave." Brown was born in 1800 and, while still a youth, he saw a Negro boy with whom he was friends badly beaten. This experience, coupled with his belief that slavery was a sin against God, strongly influenced the path of his life. He married twice, had 20 children, and lived in Pennsylvania and Ohio up until 1849. At that time he moved to New York State, to this farm, to assist in a plan formulated by Gerrit Smith, a noted New York abolitionist and philanthropist. Smith wanted to donate parcels of land to free Negroes who wished to establish farms. Brown helped these settlers in building their homes and planting their crops, but their settlement was short lived.

Brown is best known for leading an assault on the United States Arsenal at Harper's Ferry, Virginia, in 1859. The idea was to capture arms for use in the campaign to free Southern slaves. Brown was captured, convicted, and hanged for his participation in the raid. The abolitionist and two of his sons who were killed at Harper's Ferry are buried here, lemon lilies bordering their graves in the neat little cemetery protected by a black iron fence. The farmhouse, restored to its original appearance in the 1950s, is furnished in the style of a typical mid-19th-century Adirondack farmhouse.

After exploring the simple furnishings inside, ask the hostess for a free farm trail guide. The trail begins at the pond just south of the farmhouse and takes about half an hour to complete. You'll walk past zigzagging fences, through the fields, and into the woods, where tiny pine cones cover the path. The booklet identifies 12 species of trees commonly found in the Adirondacks, including the sugar maple (a source of fuel, hardwood, and maple sugar) and the yellow birch (for high-quality lumber), the spruce (popular for fence rails) and the northern white cedar (decay-resistant wood especially good for fence posts and shingles).

Just across the main road from the ski jump complex, you'll see the Lake Placid Airport, which serves as home base for the **Adirondack Flying Service.** An experienced mountain pilot will take you (minimum of two passengers) on a 20-minute scenic flight in a Cessna 172 or 206. There are two routes to choose from. The first takes you over Lake Placid Village, the Olympic venues, and Whiteface Mountain, while the second gives you a close-up of Mount Marcy, the highest point in New York State, and Lake Tear of the Clouds, the source of the Hudson River.

Continue on Route 73 into the village of Lake Placid. If you are an ice-skating enthusiast, take a look at the Speed Skating Oval located on Main

Shall we dance? Lake Placid's Olympic Arena is the home of figure skating's once and future champions.

NANCIE BATTAGLIA

Street, right in front of the Lake Placid High School. This is where legends like Eric Heiden take the gold. Then take a walk through the **Olympic Arena and Convention Center** a few steps away. The largest ice complex of its type in the world, it shelters four ice surfaces, including the 1980 Olympic Arena, site of the United States' memorable ice hockey victory over the Soviet Union. Blocks of time are set aside for public skating throughout the year, so bring along your skates. Skating shows are also held here most Saturdays. Even in the middle of summer, there's almost always a mound of snow on display out in front of the complex beneath a sign that says "It's no miracle — it's real snow."

There's almost always a mound of snow on display beneath a sign that says "It's no miracle — it's real snow."

If you want to take a break from Olympic fever, spend a little time exploring the village's lively Main Street. At the **Old Time Photo Studio** you can have your picture taken in period costumes. Dress up in an antebellum hoop skirt or parade around as a 1920s gangster. The costume collection includes accessories like fishnet stockings, feather boas, top hats, sabers, and guns, to complete your new old look. Pictures are developed on the spot, and you can even have them made into postcards or perhaps mounted on a "Wanted" poster.

Give your feet a break by taking a nostalgic horse-and-buggy tour of the village. The **Lake Placid Carriage Company** provides half-hour tours along Mirror Lake in elegant surreys (with a fringe on top). Your driver will point out local highlights, including her favorite restaurants.

If you would like to get out on Mirror Lake, stop in at **Jones Outfitter's Ltd.** Rowboats, canoes, and paddleboats can be rented here by the hour, day, or week. If you have never canoed before or have limited experience, you can join a guided daytrip. Trips depart Friday, Saturday, and Sunday mornings. Lunch and equipment rental are included in the package price; reservations are required. The route involves a short portage over to Lake Placid. You'll have the opportunity to swim and fish as well as to paddle before returning in the late afternoon. If you would rather go independently, staffers are ready to provide advice on routes and fishing spots. The quarry includes lake, brook, and rainbow trout, along with bass and perch.

If you plan to go off fishing for the day on your own, or if you need a lunch to take along on a hike, check out the edibles at **Potluck,** right on Main Street. Assemble a scrumptious picnic from fixings that include lots of imported cheeses, fresh-baked

What says summer more than a concert in the park? Stake out a piece of turf and enjoy the Lake Placid Sinfonietta.

tea cakes, and fresh salads. Sandwiches are constructed on pumpernickel, poppy-seed, rye, wheat, or white bread or an onion roll. For dessert, splurge on a couple of Champlain American Truffles, made by the Champlain Truffle Company. Each of these succulent hand-coated chocolate confections has a special filling — raspberry, amaretto praline, cappuccino, or Grand Marnier, to name just a few.

For evening entertainment in the summer, take in a musical performance by the **Lake Placid Sinfonietta.** This group originated back in 1919. Today the orchestra offers a series of free outdoor evening concerts in Village Park on Main Street (usually on Wednesday nights). Featuring well-known guest conductors, the Sinfonietta also performs regularly at the Lake Placid Center for the Arts.

There you have it — a generous sampling of Lake Placid. But be forewarned. We've only just begun to scratch the surface, revealing a few of our personal favorites. You're sure to make plenty of discoveries on your own.

Each Champlain American truffle has its own special filling — raspberry, amaretto praline, cappuccino, and Grand Marnier, to name a few.

ACCESS

LAKE PLACID. To reach Lake Placid, follow I-87 (the Northway) to Route 73. Follow Route 73 to Lake Placid.

MT. VAN HOEVENBERG RECREATION AREA. Directions: Located seven miles southeast of Lake Placid center, on Route 73. **Season:** Year round. Sliding from November to March, with bobsled rides available to the public when races are not taking place. Cross-country skiing from early December to late March. **Admission:** Charged. **Telephone:** (518) 523-4437.

OLYMPIC SKI JUMP COMPLEX. Directions: Located on Route 73, about three miles southeast of Lake Placid.

Season: Year round. **Admission:** Charged. **Telephone:** (518) 523-1655.

WHITEFACE MOUNTAIN VETERANS MEMORIAL HIGHWAY. Directions: Located just north of chairlift. **Season:** Mid-May to mid-October. **Admission:** Charged. **Telephone:** (518) 523-1655.

WHITEFACE MOUNTAIN CHAIRLIFT. Directions: From Lake Placid, follow Route 86 north nine miles to Wilmington and chairlift. **Season:** Late June through mid-October. **Admission:** Charged. **Telephone:** (518) 523-1655.

JOHN BROWN FARM. Directions: From Lake Placid Village, take Route 73 south for two miles. The farm is located on John Brown Road, about three-quarters of a mile off Route 73. **Season:** House open late May through late October. Grounds open year round. **Admission:** Free. **Telephone:** (518) 523-3900.

ADIRONDACK FLYING SERVICE. Directions: Airport is located on Route 73, opposite Olympic Ski Jump Complex. **Season:** Year round. **Admission:** Charged. **Telephone:** (518) 523-2473.

OLYMPIC ARENA AND CONVENTION CENTER. Directions: Located on Main Street in the center of Lake Placid. **Season:** Year round. **Admission:** Free. (Fees charged for public skating, shows, etc.) **Telephone:** (518) 523-3325.

OLD TIME PHOTO STUDIO. Directions: Located at 120 Main Street in the Alpine Mall. **Season:** Year round. **Admission:** Free. **Telephone:** (518) 523-1616.

LAKE PLACID CARRIAGE COMPANY. Directions: Trips depart from Main Street in the center of Lake Placid. **Season:** Memorial Day through Labor Day. **Admission:** Charged. **Telephone:** (518) 523-2483.

JONES OUTFITTER'S LTD. Directions: Located at 37 Main Street in Lake Placid. **Season:** Early May through late October. **Admission:** Free. **Telephone:** (518) 523-3468.

POTLUCK. Directions: Located on Main Street in Lake Placid. **Season:** Year round. **Admission:** Free. **Telephone:** (518) 523-3106.

LAKE PLACID SINFONIETTA. Directions: Concerts are held at various locations. **Season:** July and August. **Admission:** Charge for some events; others are free. **Note:** For schedule and ticket information, write to Lake Placid Sinfonietta, Box 1303, Lake Placid, N.Y. 12946.

For lodging and restaurant suggestions, contact the Chamber of Commerce, Lake Placid, N.Y. 12946. **Telephone:** (518) 523-2445.

Blue Mountain Lake

NANCIE BATTAGLIA

It is difficult to imagine a village more exquisitely beautiful than Blue Mountain Lake. This tiny Adirondack town is one of those infrequent jewels that manage to remain true to themselves despite the thousands of visitors who pass through during a typical season. Blue Mountain rises to a height of 3,800 feet and looks down over shimmering Blue Mountain Lake, freckled with islands and stocked with bass, whitefish, and trout. There is a small public swimming beach right in the village. There is not too much else — the post office, a couple of stores, a boat livery, a garage, a few places to eat, and the art center — yet there is plenty.

Blue Mountain Lake itself lies 1,800 feet above sea level, smack dab in the center of the Adirondack Forest Preserve and Adirondack State Park. To get a true overview, climb the 2½-mile-long trail to the top of Blue Mountain, where you'll have a view of 165 different peaks and 16 lakes. The Adirondack Forest Preserve is the heart of the Adirondack Park, one of the most unusual parks in the United States. About the same size as Vermont, the park is a network of public and private lands, some belonging to the state and others to businesses and individuals.

Need to get away from it all? There's not much action in Blue Mountain Lake, but there is beauty and serenity, as far as the eye can see.

There are about a hundred towns, villages, and hamlets within the park, populated by perhaps 120,000 year-round residents.

Several million visitors venture into the mountains, valleys, and forests each year. The Forest Preserve, which now consists of 2.5 million of the six million acres that make up the park, was created by legislative act in 1885: "The lands now or hereafter constituting the Forest Preserve shall be forever kept as wild forest lands." The combination of public and private lands gives the park a diverse mix of open space and recreational lands, summer houses and year-round villages. Use Blue Mountain Lake as your "base camp" from which to explore the surrounding countryside. Stay a day, a week, a month. Stay as long as you can.

The mountains and valleys are covered with spruce, beech, birch, and maples. Altogether there are 30 tree species native to the park. There are also hundreds of species of shrubs, wildflowers, herbs, and grasses. Wildlife abounds. Nearly 300 species of birds live here, unusual ones like the fisher, American marten, golden eagle, and spruce grouse. There are 64 species of mammals, including white-tailed deer, black bear, and moose, as well as 35 types of reptiles and amphibians and 82 species of fish. All of this flora and fauna is easily accessible from Blue Mountain Lake.

To orient yourself to the region, and to get a sense of its history and folklore, spend half a day at **The Adirondack Museum.** Truly one of a kind, this indoor/outdoor museum is tucked neatly between Blue Mountain Lake and Blue Mountain, affording nearly constant glimpses of both. There are 20 exhibit buildings to explore, some simple and some extensive. You'll want to begin in the main building, which contains exhibits highlighting the land and the history of the region. Get your bearings by examining the large pushbutton map, which allows you to illuminate specific towns, rivers, mountains, and lakes in the huge park.

Take a look at the detailed series of dioramas, each one accompanied by a "hearphone," a headset that dispenses an explanatory narrative about the scene before you. You'll learn that the Adirondack Cottage Sanitarium opened by Dr. Edward L. Trudeau in 1885 made nearby Saranac Lake a center for the study and treatment of tuberculosis. A detailed model of a loggers' cookhouse provides an intimate look at the "men's room" (off-limits to women), where 19th-century lumberjacks smoked, talked,

The 40 loggers in the camp dispensed with 400 eggs, three whole hams, and innumerable loaves of bread in a single sitting.

Seated viewers watch old photos from the Adirondack Museum's vast collection pass before their very eyes on the Photo Belt.

and played cards. At one camp, the crew of 40 loggers were known to have dispensed with 400 eggs, three whole hams, and innumerable loaves of bread in a single sitting.

You'll visit a log hotel built in 1876 and you'll see what kinds of accommodations were available in the Adirondacks between 1850 and 1940, including a model of a typical middle-class hotel room complete with pitcher and basin and a crazy quilt on the oak bedstead. Very cosy! Writing in 1873, one visitor observed that "there were games of croquet on the lawn, boating parties upon the lake, lovers sauntering in the woods, and a Chickering thrumming in the parlor."

"Woods and Waters: Outdoor Recreation in the Adirondacks" is a worthy museum in its own right. On entering this enormous building, you'll pass through simulated outdoor settings — walking across a stream on a rustic bridge, following a trail into the woods. You'll come to a simple lean-to with water rushing by and a campfire blazing, birds chirping in the night, a canoe pulled up on the shore. There are lots of angling artifacts and a slide show that touches on logging, surveying, and stagecoach travel. You'll pass the hermit's cabin, and hear an old radio interview made with its one-time occupant, Noah John Rondeau.

Displays on trapping show otter, bobcat, bear, and other pelts, along with animal traps, early snowshoes, and eight graceful wooden toboggans and sleds, including one that belonged to a city milkman. There's an 1890 hearse, too, with wheels for summer and runners for winter, complete with removal basket, that was used by the Barton Funeral Home for over 70 years. If you admire fine craftsmanship, you'll marvel over the 800 wooden miniatures made by one local man — everything from an elegant circus wagon to a tiny footstool to 407 chairs with no two the same.

One 19th-century visitor recalled "games of croquet on the lawn, boating parties upon the lake, and a Chickering thrumming in the parlor."

You'll marvel over the 800 wooden miniatures made by one local man — everything from an elegant circus wagon to a tiny footstool.

From patchwork to padding, supplies to finished treasures, Blue Mountain Designs has everything for lovers of the fabric arts.

COURTESY BLUE MOUNTAIN DESIGNS

Another section of this building that never seems to end is devoted to waterways, the principal arteries of travel and transport through the mountains from spring thaw to winter freeze, right up until the construction of the railroad and hard-surfaced roadways. Here you'll see examples of the famous Adirondack guideboat with its caned seat, along with the wherry, bateau, and dory that were built to meet the needs of hunters, fishermen, loggers, and tourists.

We've barely begun to scratch the surface of what the museum has to offer. There are early 20th-century boats in the boat pond, including the steamboat *Osprey* and the excursion launch *Mountaineer.* Separate buildings are devoted to logging and to mining. And there is even a long photo belt where you can take a seat and watch historic photographs pass by. By the time you leave, you will know a little about subjects as diverse as environmental conservation and the rustic furniture made for service in Adirondack work camps. This is a museum that truly gives a sense of the people who were drawn to the Adirondacks and the kinds of lives they led.

Blue Mountain has only 150 year-round residents, yet it is also the home of **The Adirondack Lakes Center for the Arts,** which offers courses in many different crafts and presents plays, concerts, and films. Nearly 200,000 people have attended the programs since the center opened in 1967. There is a crafts shop where you can pick up handmade toys, baskets, pottery, prints, and other special things made by regional artists and craftsmen. You might be in for a banjo concert or an evening of early music or fiery jazz. Or perhaps you are interested in the documentary film series. There are also lots of films and workshops especially for children. Intensive one- and two-day workshops are scheduled in photography, printmaking, weaving, calligraphy, woodworking, stained glass, basketry, batik, welding, drawing, painting, pottery, and other crafts, for children and adults, beginners to experts.

Just a few yards down the road from the center, you can visit **Blue Mountain Designs,** a craft gallery that specializes in fabric arts. This is also a good place to stock up on quilting supplies and fabrics.

Guides are an old tradition in the Adirondacks, and you might want to consider engaging the services of one for an unforgettable outdoor experience. **Blue Mountain Lake Guide Service** offers four different types of adventure. You can spend the day rafting the Hudson River Gorge, traveling through 15 tumultuous miles of almost continuous whitewater during the spring runoff. You'll be provided with everything you need, from licensed guide, wetsuit, life jacket, and paddles to lunch on the river and a ride from Blue Mountain Lake village to and from the river. For a less demanding but perhaps even more beautiful trip (if that's possible), sign on for the same route during a fall weekend when the foliage is at its peak and the river is much gentler. The service also organizes six-day hunts with a wood-heated tent and base camp for groups of six hunters. A team of two people can sign up a guide for a fishing trip, via canoe or rowboat, on a secluded stream or pond. You'll have fresh trout or bass for supper that night. What could be a more fitting finale to a day in the Adirondacks?

Tackle the 15 tumultuous miles of almost continuous whitewater during the spring runoff.

ACCESS

BLUE MOUNTAIN LAKE. Follow I-90 (New York State Thruway) to Exit 27. Take Route 30 north to Blue Mountain Lake, bearing left at the Route 28 intersection.

THE ADIRONDACK MUSEUM. Directions: Located one mile north of Blue Mountain Lake on Route 30. **Season:** Mid-June through mid-October. **Admission:** Charged. **Telephone:** (518) 352-7311.

THE ADIRONDACK LAKES CENTER FOR THE ARTS. Directions: Located on Route 28 in Blue Mountain Lake. **Season:** Year round. **Admission:** Free. Fees for performances and workshops. **Telephone:** (518) 352-7715.

BLUE MOUNTAIN DESIGNS. Directions: Located on Route 30 in Blue Mountain Lake. **Season:** May through October. **Admission:** Free. **Telephone:** (518) 352-7361.

BLUE MOUNTAIN LAKE GUIDE SERVICE. Directions: For trip information, write to the service at Box 111, Blue Mountain Lake, N.Y. 12812. **Season:** April through late October. **Admission:** Trip fees. **Telephone:** (518) 352-7684.

For information on the **Adirondack Park,** write to the Department of Environmental Conservation, Bureau of Recreation and Field Operation, Room 619, 50 Wolf Road, Albany, N.Y. 12233. **Telephone:** (518) 457-2500.

For lodging and restaurant suggestions, write to Hamilton County Publicity, Long Lake, N.Y. 12847. **Telephone:** (518) 624-4151.

Cooperstown

Say "Cooperstown" and nine out of 10 people will respond, "Baseball Hall of Fame." They'd be right, of course. Cooperstown certainly is the home of **The National Baseball Hall of Fame and Museum,** but there are also lots of other reasons to visit. The town was founded by Judge William Cooper, the father of author James Fenimore Cooper (who made it the setting for his now classic "Leatherstocking Tales"). Today this orderly village is a resort that doesn't really feel or look like a resort. It is charming, it is quaint, but it isn't cute. To put it bluntly, Cooperstown has class. Add to that illusive quality a lovely pastoral setting nestled up against shimmery Lake Otsego and you begin to understand what makes it so special.

Cooperstown calls itself New York's "Village of Museums," and for good reason. Let's start with the Hall of Fame, the magnet that initially draws so many visitors. Begin in the Cooperstown Room, where a videotape recalls nostalgic moments in baseball history when legendary players like Babe Ruth, Ty Cobb, and Honus Wagner were inducted into the Hall of Fame. You'll see Willie Mays remi-

Ty Cobb and Cy Young, two of the legendary players enshrined at the Baseball Hall of Fame in Cooperstown.

NATIONAL BASEBALL HALL OF FAME AND MUSEUM

nisce about the advice offered to him as a rookie by manager Leo Durocher: "Son, you don't have to hit. Just go out there and catch the ball."

You'll also hear the popular account of Abner Doubleday starting the game of baseball in Farmer Phinney's Cooperstown pasture, where his home-made baseball (now displayed in the museum) was later discovered. The game attributed to Doubleday eventually led to the creation of a new set of American heroes.

In the 1870s baseball players wore fingerless leather pads, sometimes on both hands.

The actual Hall of Fame is a cavernous room with high ceilings and marble columns. A plaque capsulizes the history of each of baseball's recognized immortals — the teams each played for and the records each set — but most intriguing are the additional remarks, which give real insight into the history of our national pastime. Take Harold Henry "Pee Wee" Reese, for example. "Shortstop and captain of great Dodger teams of 1940s and '50s. Intangible qualities of subtle leadership and off-field competitive fire and professional pride. Complemented dependable glove with reliable base-running and clutch hitting as significant factors in seven Dodger pennants. Instrumental in easing acceptance of Jackie Robinson as baseball's first black performer."

Displays in the Great Moments Room document famous pitching duels, no-hitters, perfect games, and legendary hitting streaks. There are four floors of displays altogether. One set of exhibits chronicles the evolution of bats, balls, and gloves. You'll discover that players started out using their bare hands. In the 1870s they wore fingerless leather pads, sometimes on both hands. Eventually they added fingers, with webbing between the thumb and fingers to help catch the ball.

Did you know that batting crowns really exist? You'll see them here, gold with red velvet, bejeweled and engraved. Other artifacts are as varied as Babe Ruth's locker from Yankee Stadium (complete with his shaving brush, uniform, bats, and glove) and an original seat from Ebbets Field. There are exhibits devoted to the history of the ballpark, all-star games, the World Series, and even minor league and youth baseball. The baseball card collection includes the rarest card of them all, the Honus Wagner card produced by Sweet Caporal Tobacco Company between 1909 and 1911. The card was recalled because Wagner didn't smoke and he objected to the use of his picture in promoting tobacco products. A visit to the Hall of Fame pro-

Artifacts include Babe Ruth's locker and an original seat from Ebbets Field.

vides insight into a slice of all-American social history, and that's why it's fun even for folks who don't really think of themselves as baseball fans.

When you leave the museum, stop by **Doubleday Field,** a block and a half down Main Street. The annual Hall of Fame Game is played here at the world's first baseball diamond each summer. Originally built for 8,000 spectators, and later expanded to accommodate 10,000, it's a batter's park, with a short 297-foot left field and a 312-foot right field line. Kids find it thrilling to run the bases on the field where baseball got its official start over a century ago.

Right next to the field, you can show off your skills at the **Doubleday Batting Range,** which is equipped with Tru-Pitch pitching machines, the same ones used by the major leagues. Each machine is capable of 17 different types of pitches. Helmets and bats are provided, and younger boys and girls can try their luck on a machine that pitches yellow tennis balls. Older, more seasoned players will want to try making contact with a 40 mph knuckleball or a 50 mph overhand curve. And the truly insane can always opt for a 65 mph screwball. There's a softball batting cage, too. The batting range even offers a radar pitching-speed recorder with a digital readout that tells you just how fast you can pitch.

Hungry from all that exercise? Here are three refueling stops, all strung out along Main Street within a two-minute walk of the batting range. **Schneider's Bakery** has glass cases full of homemade cookies and pastries. Our favorites are the enormous flaky "elephant ears." The breads are delicious, too, particularly the pumpernickel with raisins. **The Shortstop** serves "breakfast anytime." This unpretentious coffee shop dishes up something also called The Shortstop, consisting of ham, egg, and melted cheese served on an English muffin, made to order.

For fancier fare, try **The Market Place.** Bring your own picnic basket or purchase one here, then have it filled with unusual sandwiches. Choices include the Mulberry Street Special (genoa salami, capicollo, sliced pepperoni, imported provolone, Bermuda onion, anchovies, tomato, basil, and homemade Italian dressing on a hard roll) or a Scandia Special (wine-cured filet of herring with dill pickle and sour cream on pumpernickel). Or opt for a croissant stuffed with crabmeat or homemade chicken salad. There are individual packages of imported biscuits and cookies and scrumptious Italian,

Seasoned batters try their hand at making contact with a 40 mph knuckleball or a 50 mph overhand curve.

All aboard for a wagon ride through the Village Crossroads and a journey back to 19th-century America.

French, and Greek pastries for dessert. If you prefer to eat here, sit down at one of the butcher block tables under the red awning in the café area. In addition to gourmet sandwiches, the menu lists homemade soups and salads and several hot Italian specialties like linguine with white clam sauce and tortellini Alfredo. Open 9 A.M. to 9 P.M. daily, the year round, this is a good place to keep in mind for breakfast, lunch, or supper.

For a taste of Lake Otsego, immortalized as "Glimmerglass Lake" in Cooper's "Leatherstocking Tales," take a cruise aboard the *Chief Uncas*, operated by **Lake Otsego Boat Tours.** Built in 1912 for the Busch family of Budweiser beer fame, the elegant mahogany launch holds up to 30 passengers. The crew will tell stories about points of interest along the one-hour route — places like Council Rock, Natty Bumppo's Cave, and Sunken Island.

The two other major museums in the village are the **Fenimore House** and the **Farmers' Museum and Village Crossroads,** both of which are managed by the New York State Historical Association. Located on the grounds of Cooper's Fenimore Farm, the elegant **Fenimore Museum** houses many pieces of furniture and works of art associated with Judge William Cooper and his son James Fenimore Cooper. Two additional floors contain an outstanding collection of American folk art, from trade signs, weathervanes, and decoys to decorated furniture, fireboards, and theorem paintings.

Among the pictures, we found the genre paintings particularly fascinating. These record commonplace activities and life experiences in a realistic manner. The attention to detail is so precise that paintings like *Van Bergen Overmantel*, a detailed oil-on wood scene of a Hudson Valley Dutch farm, are as much historical documents as works of art. You will also see a version of Edward Hicks' famous painting, *Peaceable Kingdom*. Probably the best known of the 19th-century primitive painters,

Hicks was a Quaker minister who used his favorite Bible passage, "the lion shall lie down with the lamb," as the theme for nearly a hundred paintings.

Hicks was a Quaker minister who used his favorite Biblical passage, "the lion shall lie down with the lamb," as the theme for nearly a hundred peaceable kingdom paintings. Together with the wealth of primitive portraits, these paintings provide a pre-photographic visual record of what people did, what they wore, and the objects they used.

At the **Farmers' Museum and Village Crossroads,** you'll become acquainted with a century of change in upstate New York. The exhibits begin with a look at the simple frontier farm and move on to the prospering farm of the 1850s, when the farmer enjoyed the luxury of having surplus grains to sell. It took the average farmer about 10 years to clear 30 to 40 acres of land and to build a barn and a large house to replace the original log cabins. The main museum building contains exhibits that illuminate many aspects of rural life, from fence construction to planting techniques, trapping to basketmaking. Here and there a contemporary craftsman demonstrates a traditional technique, be it cabinetmaking or broom manufacture.

Out behind the museum, the Village Crossroads is actually a living-history museum. Sheep graze on the common and there are horseshoe prints in the mud from a team pulling a wagon through the village. Hitch a ride, or take a walk along the dirt road. Drop in at the print shop to pick up a broadside, or take a break at the general store to play a game of checkers. The cows in the nearby fields wear low-pitched, clanking bells, and you'll hear them before you see them. Chickens and geese go about their business, scratching and honking, and a calf with a sandpaper tongue sucks on your fingers as you reach into its pen to give it a scratch behind the ears. As you explore the village, you'll learn how 19th-century farmers managed their lives and how they handled chores as diverse as digging a well and making clothing. There are often special events in progress, too. The day we visited we had a chance to try our luck at rolling a wooden hoop, balancing on stilts, and playing 19th-century games like "put and take" and "graces."

There is so much to do in Cooperstown and the setting is so serene that you may well want to stay overnight. If you visit during the summer, you can treat yourself to a performance of the **Cooperstown Theatre Festival,** the only professional equity theater company in the area. Performances are staged in a charming Victorian theater a few miles north of Cooperstown. There is a café here, too, where you

Craftspeople at the Farmers' Museum give visitors an up-close glimpse of 19th-century technologies at work.

can have a light supper or just a glass of wine, to round out a most pleasant evening in Leatherstocking country.

ACCESS

COOPERSTOWN. To reach Cooperstown, follow I-88 to Route 28 north into the center of town.

THE NATIONAL BASEBALL HALL OF FAME AND MUSEUM. Directions: Entering town on Route 28, turn right on Main Street. Hall of Fame will be on your right. **Season:** Year round. **Admission:** Charged. **Telephone:** (607) 547-9988.

DOUBLEDAY FIELD. Directions: Located on Main Street near the Hall of Fame. **Season:** Year round. **Admission:** Free. **Telephone:** None.

DOUBLEDAY BATTING RANGE. Directions: Located next to Doubleday Field, off Main Street. **Season:** Memorial Day through Columbus Day. **Admission:** Free. **Telephone:** (607) 547-5168.

SCHNEIDER'S BAKERY. Directions: Located at the corner of Main Street and Route 28/80. **Season:** Year round. **Admission:** Free. **Telephone:** (607) 547-9631.

THE SHORTSTOP. Directions: Located on Main Street near the Hall of Fame. **Season:** Year round. **Admission:** Free. **Telephone:** (607) 547-9609.

THE MARKET PLACE. Directions: Located at 93 Main Street. **Season:** Year round. **Admission:** Free. **Telephone:** (607) 547-5468.

LAKE OTSEGO BOAT TOURS. Directions: Ticket office at pier adjacent to Lakefront Park. **Season:** May through mid-October. **Admission:** Charged. **Telephone:** (607) 547-5295.

FENIMORE MUSEUM. Directions: Located on Route 80, just north of the center of town. **Season:** May through December. **Admission:** Charged. **Telephone:** (607) 547-2533.

FARMERS' MUSEUM AND VILLAGE CROSS-ROADS. Directions: Located on Route 80, just north of the center of town. **Season:** April through December. **Admission:** Charged. **Telephone:** (607) 547-2533.

COOPERSTOWN THEATRE FESTIVAL. Directions: Theater is located on Route 80, seven miles north of Cooperstown. **Season:** Late June through September 1. **Admission:** Charged. **Telephone:** (607) 547-2335.

For restaurant and lodging suggestions, contact the Cooperstown Chamber of Commerce at 31 Chestnut Street, P.O. Box 46, Cooperstown, N.Y. 13326. **Telephone:** (607) 547-9983.

N.Y. STATE HISTORICAL ASSOCIATION, COOPERSTOWN

Picking Flowers, *an oil painting attributed to Samuel Miller, is an example of the wealth of primitives on display at the Fenimore Museum.*

Utica

Back in the early days of our country's settlement, stalwart frontiersmen lugging muskets and wearing protective leather leggings made their way along the Mohawk Trail. Utica, which developed near the western terminus of the trail, is located in that part of the state called the "central leatherstocking section," named in honor of those rugged individuals. An industrial center with a tradition of manufacturing and commercial trade that stretches back to the 1700s, contemporary Utica is tinged with nostalgia and accented by small-town friendliness. It seems only fitting that the very first Woolworth five-and-dime store opened its doors here in 1879.

A visit to the **F.X. Matt Brewing Company** will quickly clarify the combination of ingredients that characterizes the city: the busy tempo of an urban manufacturing center, a strong sense of history, and old-fashioned hospitality. You'll be greeted by a costumed "Gibson Girl" in the restored Victorian reception center, with its circular red velvet banquettes, stained glass, flocked wallpaper, and heavy

COURTESY F.X. MATT BREWERY

Imagine a recipe that calls for adding hops to an 18,000-gallon copper kettle! The F.X. Matt Brewery keeps two such kettles going all the time.

green drapes. Company president F.X. Matt II makes a complete inspection of the plant each day, and you just may run into him as you tour the brewery that his grandfather, the original F.X. Matt, began back in 1888. Many of the people who work in the plant today are descendants of people who worked for the founder, making this in every way a family business.

Your guide will lead you into the warm, sweet-smelling brewhouse, where two mammoth copper kettles hold up to 18,000 gallons of beer at one time. You'll learn how corn, rice, and malt are combined, filtered, then piped into kettles in a brewing process that takes about 10 hours. Then move on to the glass-lined refrigerated tanks, where Matt's Premium ferments for seven days before continuing on to the next step in the process: aging. You'll shiver as you walk through the quarry-tiled glass enclosure adjoining the aging cellars, where the temperature is always kept below 40 degrees Fahrenheit. (If you consumed 10 beers a day, it would take you 88 years to drink the contents of one of these tanks.)

In the bottling works, you'll see bottles washed, filled, capped, pasteurized, and labeled. They march along conveyor belts like well-trained soldiers, and when the plant is operating at full capacity, 2.4 million can be processed in a single day. The beer is distributed mostly within a 200-mile radius of Utica, making it one of those regional food specialties you really ought to sample. That's easy to do, because at the end of the tour the red and green Utica Club trolley with the gold velvet curtains will transport you to a restored 1888 tavern, where you can enjoy a foaming mug of Matt's Premium Beer (or a root beer, if you prefer), compliments of the house. Bartenders in black vests slide glass mugs down the counter of the ornately carved wooden bar with the brass footrail while the nickelodeon plays enthusiastically. When you're refreshed, you can head for the gift shop, which peddles all sorts of reproduction Victorian memorabilia. You can also pick up an unusual souvenir here, a mixed case of Matt's beers: Matt's Light, Matt's Premium, Maximus Super, and Utica Club.

Only a few minutes' drive from the brewery, experience quite another facet of Utica at the **Munson-Williams-Proctor Institute,** which includes an art museum and a house museum, as well as an art school and a comprehensive performing arts program. The 25-year-old museum is housed in a dramatic Classical-style building cited in 1962 by the

If you consumed 10 beers a day, it would take you 88 years to drink the contents of one of these tanks.

The nickelodeon plays enthusiastically as bartenders in black vests slide glass mugs down the ornately carved wooden bar.

GALE FARLEY/MUNSON-WILLIAMS-PROCTOR INSTITUTE

editors of *Architectural Forum* as one of 10 new buildings worldwide that contributed significantly to the developing art of architecture.

The museum collection consists of over 5,000 paintings, drawings, prints, sculptures, and pieces of decorative art, most of them American. Be sure to climb up to the balcony for a look at the famous "Voyage of Life" series of early 19th-century artist Thomas Cole, probably the most important member of the Hudson River School of landscape painters. This series of huge canvases allegorizes man's passage through the four stages of life: childhood, youth, manhood, and old age. Landscape motifs like rivers and caves, mountains and waterfalls are woven through paintings that parallel man's journey through life with the passing of the seasons.

Ladies once used fire screens to keep their makeup from melting, and slipper chairs for putting on their high-button shoes.

One small but important point we'd like to make is that this museum really understands the difficulties in appreciating an art collection with youngsters in tow. Kids three to 10 years old are welcome to stay in an attractive, supervised children's room while their parents go off and tour the galleries. There are enticing toys to play with, as well as four work stations where kids can experiment, using plastic pieces to create different patterns on illuminated boards.

On leaving the museum, stop in at the **Fountain Elms,** right next door. The Victorian Italianate villa was the home of Proctor and Munson family members and contains many of their possessions. The decor and furnishings reflect mid-19th-century social customs. There are fire screens used by the ladies to keep their makeup from melting, and slipper chairs for putting on their high-button shoes. The dining room has a French Empire-style clock depicting Cupid riding in a lion-drawn chariot. From the French gilt-bronze chandeliers to the massive Empire bed to the ornately carved John Belter sofa and étagère, the house is filled with treasures that reflect the excesses of the period. Visits are by guided tour only, but the tours are informal and the guides appear eager to address the visitor's interests.

Now make a side trip to the town of Deansboro to visit **The Musical Museum,** where you can crank, pump, and play restored melodeons, nickelodeons, early phonographs, grind organs, and more. The single-story, rambling building that houses the collection doesn't look very impressive from the outside, but within you'll find 17 rooms stuffed full of music-making machines, many of which you can activate. As you enter, you will probably be greeted by the sounds of the Violano-Virtuoso, which mechanically combines the sounds of a piano and two violins. About 2,500 of these magnet-controlled music machines were produced by the Mills Company of Chicago in the early 1900s.

Visitors are first treated to a brief demonstration, showing off some of the museum's rarest treasures. We could feel the vibrations as six tiny birds struck a bell and two little dancers in red and green silk dresses twirled on the surface of a single-cylinder Swiss music box dating back to 1878. The 48-tune box took two years to make and originally sold for 75 dollars. We also heard "Take Me Out to the Ball Game," courtesy of an 1897 Regina music box. Today the Regina company manufactures electric brooms and vacuum cleaners, but back then they made early jukeboxes like this one: a penny a tune or six for a nickel. We also listened to a pair of French mechanical birds in a gilded cage imitate the mockingbird and cardinal, while flapping their wings.

After the demonstration, wander through the maze of rooms crammed with classic music makers like the hurdy-gurdys, automatic player pianos, and the coinola, which combines a snare drum rule, bass drum, cymbal, xylophone, mandolin reeds, triangle, and timpani, all of which you can see in action right above the keyboard. There's even a Mississippi steamboat organ. When you put a quarter in the Orchestrion, a curtain opens, revealing violinist, bass player, drummer, and trumpeter, all swaying to the music.

Allow at least an hour for your visit. If you're a nostalgia buff and tunes like "My Wild Irish Rose" or "Boogie-Woogie Bugle Boy" take you way back,

Six tiny birds strike a bell and two little dancers in red and green silk dresses twirl on the surface of a 48-tune Swiss music box.

When you put a quarter in the Orchestrion, a curtain opens, revealing tiny musicians swaying to the music.

you'll want to stay much longer. One room is set up as a traditional soda fountain, and you can sit down at a table and drink a lemonade while you listen to the Wurlitzers and Seeburgs belt out Benny Goodman and Glenn Miller numbers. If you want to take some of the fun home, check out the selection of LPs available in the gift shop, recordings of the restored instruments in the museum.

In traveling from Utica to Deansboro the back way (via Route 12, then left on Route 315 in Waterville), we inadvertently came upon Clinton, a charming college town. Here we met Jonathan Woodward, proprietor and resident potter of **Woodward's,** a gracious studio/gallery/shop located right across from the town common. The building used to be part of a hotel catering to the affluent. "It was super-duper swanky," Jonathan explained. His gallery has a high tin ceiling, shiny maple flooring cast off from a local school gymnasium, track lighting, and walls of bare brick and plain white. There is no clutter here, just light and space, the perfect backdrop for Woodward's own handsome pottery as well as other exquisite objects, like the wooden music stands and a cherry bureau made by top-notch cabinetmaker Steven MacKintosh. We also found African baskets, English cosmetics, a few choice pieces of sculpture, some greeting cards, and several paintings. Everything is in the best of taste. Woodward's studio is right behind the gallery area, and he doesn't mind a bit if you watch him work. More like a congenial host than a shopkeeper, he makes a visit to his gallery an absolutely lovely experience.

Just a couple of doors down from Woodward's, you can get a bite to eat at **The Village Green,** a self-service restaurant featuring homemade soups, chile, and sandwiches. Opt for a hot dog with sauerkraut, chile, onions, and cheese — or maybe a grilled reuben — and settle into one of the commodious booths.

At Jonathan Woodward's suggestion, we made a stop at **The Root Glen,** a seven-acre wooded garden and ravine belonging to Hamilton College. Along with many kinds of flowers and shrubs, the glen contains 55 species of trees. A mile of red shale pathway winds through the garden, leading to areas like the Primrose Basin and the Hemlock Enclosure, with its collection of peonies. The anemones, azaleas, and star magnolia come into bloom in April, followed by the bluebells, columbine, lilacs, peonies, and many other flowers in May. The

A red shale pathway leads to the Primrose Basin and the Hemlock Enclosure, with its collection of peonies.

irises and primroses come into their glory in June, followed by phlox, touch-me-not, and lobelia in July. September brings witch hazel and turtlehead. Squirrels and chipmunks dart over the paths as you walk through the glen, where 75 species of birds have been spotted through the years. It is a beautiful, tranquil place — the perfect spot for an evening walk, drawing to its close a lovely day.

Expect the unexpected at the Musical Museum in Deansboro.

ACCESS

UTICA. Take I-90 (New York State Thruway) to Exit 31, Utica.

F.X. MATT BREWING COMPANY. Directions: Follow I-90 (New York State Thruway) to Exit 31. From toll booth, follow I-790 to Court Street. Turn right on Court Street and continue to tour entrance, on your right. **Season:** Year round, except Sundays. Tours by reservation only from September through May. **Admission:** Free. **Telephone:** (315) 732-0022.

MUNSON-WILLIAMS-PROCTOR INSTITUTE. Directions: The museum is located at 310 Genesee Street in Utica. **Fountain Elms** is located next door. **Season:** Year round. **Admission:** Free. **Telephone:** (315) 797-0000.

THE MUSICAL MUSEUM. Directions: From I-90 (New York State Thruway), take Exit 32. Turn right, then left onto Route 233 south. Continue seven miles to junction of Route 12B. Turn right on 12B and continue three miles into Deansboro to museum entrance. **Season:** April through December. **Admission:** Charged. **Telephone:** (315) 841-8774.

WOODWARD'S. Directions: The gallery is located at 10 West Park Row, bordering the town common in the center of Clinton. **Season:** Year round. **Admission:** Free. **Telephone:** (315) 853-6873.

THE VILLAGE GREEN. Directions: Located a few doors from Woodward's on West Park Row. **Season:** Year round. **Admission:** Free. **Telephone:** None.

THE ROOT GLEN. Directions: From the center of Clinton, follow College Street to the top of the hill. Entrance to parking area will be on your left, adjacent to a large yellow house. **Season:** Year round. **Admission:** Free. **Telephone:** None.

For lodging and restaurant suggestions, contact the Convention and Visitors Bureau, 209 Elizabeth Street, Utica, N.Y. 13501. **Telephone:** (315) 724-3151.

Rome

Plunked down just about in the center of the state, Rome is likely to be one of those cities you frequently pass on your way to somewhere else. You might see the signs en route to the Thousand Islands, Niagara Falls, or the Finger Lakes region. It is not a beautiful city, nor is it the sort of destination one would choose as a vacation base. Yet we think Rome is the ideal place to take a break from your travels to more distant points. It offers a pleasant variety of activities, and it also offers a glimpse at a very important event in our country's history — the construction of the great Erie Canal.

As you drive along the New York State Thruway, you'll catch glimpses of the famous canal and its locks. Approaching Rome, you'll see **Canal Park,** the site of lock E20. There are a few picnic tables and grills here, along with an observation platform that you can climb for a good close-up view of the huge lock.

At **Erie Canal Village,** you'll learn why and how the original canal was constructed and what life was like back in the days when men shoveled the great ditch by hand. Begin your visit to this re-created 19th-century village by watching the 15-minute orientation film. You'll hear about "the great carry," a two-mile stretch of land linking the Mohawk River to the Great Lakes, the east to the west. The Indians and traders carried their boats across this expanse, which was also referred to as "a bridge across a continent." The British and the French fought with each other and with the Indians for control of the land. The idea of building a connecting waterway was the subject of much discussion, even in the 1700s. New York State's Governor Morris observed in 1777 that "At no very distant day, the waters of the great western seas will, by the aid of man, break through their barriers and mingle with those of the Hudson."

A relatively slender strip of land, the Great Carry was at one time referred to as "a bridge across a continent."

Some 40 years later, the mayor of New York City, DeWitt Clinton, showed himself a staunch proponent of a great canal project. He ran for governor in 1817 on a pro-canal platform and scored an overwhelming victory. The canal became known as "Clinton's Ditch." Using shovels, picks, and muscle, men gradually gave substance to a dream, incorporating a total of 83 locks for regulating the water

Shove off for a trip on the old Erie Canal aboard an authentic mule-drawn packet boat.

level. From the moment the canal opened, traffic was a problem. The famous ditch cost six million dollars to build; by 1882, 42 million dollars in tolls had been collected.

The village sits in a rural setting very close to the spot where the first shovelful of dirt was turned over. More than a dozen 19th-century buildings have been moved here, and they include a museum with pushbutton exhibits, like a map that lights up to show where the locks are and a recording of "Grand Canal" played on a wooden flute. You can enter the women's quarters on a packet boat, one of the stylish horse- or mule-drawn boats that carried travelers along the canal. Red velvet curtains add a touch of elegance to the three-tier bunks, suspended by leather straps. If you like early vehicles, you'll love the Harden Carriage Museum with its collection of buggies, sleighs, runabouts, and equipment like the ox-drawn snowplow used to keep the logging roads open. There's even a hearse made by a man who died from the plague, but recovered later on after a trip to the cemetery. Now you figure that one out.

Stop in at Bennet's Tavern for root beer, pretzels, and pickled eggs. Eat them in the taproom or settle down in one of the rocking chairs on the front porch, overlooking the village. Watch the blacksmith at work in his shop and then stop in at the schoolhouse, the church, and the homes. Head for the restored train station and take a 20-minute ride on the Rome and Ft. Bull Railroad, behind a half-scale steam locomotive. The biggest treat, however, is a 45-minute ride on a 1½-mile section of the canal, aboard the *Independence*, a genuine oak packet boat pulled by a team of mules.

At the nearby **Fort Rickey Game Farm,** children and animals commune up close. This attractive farm is spread out over a broad expanse of lawns and wooded groves. It is well kept and uncrowded, a relaxed, unhurried place where grown-ups feel free to relax in the afternoon sun after a picnic brought from home, while kids take another look at the resident beasts. The cast of characters includes the American bison, bear, reindeer, geese, a donkey, a porcupine, and rabbits. There's a reptile house too. Scolding and squealing monkeys swing on an island in the small pond near the main entrance. Prairie dogs appear and disappear unpredictably in their sandy enclosure, while a lion cub takes a brief nap nearby.

The biggest hit at the farm, however, is the petting area. To start with, it's very large and there's a pond across one end. The animals here, unlike those at other petting farms we've visited, seem to like their visitors. Maybe that's because there's an off-limits-to-people path leading to the grassy area behind the water, which they can take to whenever they need to get away from us all. Or maybe it's because there's so much room to spread out and so many of them to pet that they don't feel intimidated by their human visitors.

The glory of the contact area is in the number and ages of animals there are to meet. One small boy was absolutely astounded when he put his hand against the side of a pregnant goat and felt her babies move. There were a couple of young reindeer with furry antlers who were a big hit, too, along with dozens of goats and deer, some only a week or two old.

One warning is in order, however. You can buy an ice cream cone filled with seeds and corn to feed the animals, but watch out with small children. These critters can be mighty aggressive about getting their fair share, and while one toddler was stoic when a young goat put its hooves on his shoulders, another found it downright terrifying. There are pony rides available, and they might be a better investment than animal food for some kids.

One small boy was absolutely astounded when he put his hand against the side of a pregnant goat and felt her babies move.

Back in the center of Rome, absorb another facet of area history at **Fort Stanwix National Monument.** This fort is located along what was once the primary portage (remember the "great carry"?) between the Great Lakes and river access to the Atlantic Ocean. The British built Fort Stanwix in 1758, during the French and Indian War. The fort was occupied by Continental troops in 1777, when the British forces under General John Burgoyne and Colonel Barry St. Leger began a major invasion of New York State. The British laid siege to the fort for three weeks before retreating to Canada.

The National Park Service has reconstructed the fort and staffed it with costumed interpreters, who provide a lively look at life in a military outpost during the American Revolution. The day we visited, the resident surgeon was holding forth at his white medical tent near the drawbridge by the fort entrance. Laudanum, he explained, was used as a painkiller for minor operations, "like amputation of an arm or leg." For fever and infection, he preferred to let blood with a lancet or leeches. "If you have a headache," he explained, "it's because you have too much blood in your body."

Siege, a filmed drama retelling the story of the famous three-week siege, is shown in the visitor center. "Here in upstate New York," the narrator begins, "men won by simply standing fast." While cannons pound the walls, we become acquainted with the occupants of the fort, who must simply wait and see. Their voices belie their fears and frustrations: "As long as I live, I never get used to a scalping. . . . Dear Lord, would you tell them to stop the shooting so we can get some sleep?"

Wandering through the fort, we come upon soldiers going about their business. We shudder in the long, dark corridor leading to the southwest bombproof, which was used as a hospital during the siege. We enter the staff room, where the officer of the day questions us on our business ("Are you a spy?"). We visit the commandant's quarters, with its tiny canopied bed, writing desk, skin rug, jugs, and other accouterments. We become familiar with terms like parapet, redoubt, ravelin, and fraise.

The fort also contains a museum housing authentic period artifacts. There are lead game counters used in draughts (checkers) and other gambling games. There are buttons, belt buckles, and straight pins, shards of creamware and Delftware, and other touches of domestic life, many

Continental troops held strategic Fort Stanwix against a three-week British siege in 1777.

Laudanum, the surgeon explained, was used as a painkiller for minor operations, "like amputation of an arm or a leg."

of them unearthed when the fort was reconstructed. There is also a brief slide show that describes the research and building involved in the reconstruction process.

Your appetite for history satisfied, don't leave Rome without taking advantage of a contemporary phenomenon, the factory outlet store. There are several in the area, but the most popular seems to be the **Revere Ware Factory Store,** which is fitting since Rome is known for its copper and brass products. Copper-clad or stainless steel, you can choose from a full line of products, all sold well below retail. Saucepans are available in sizes that vary from one cup to 20 quarts! Expect to get as much as 50 percent off if you find what you need among the slight irregulars and factory close-outs.

ACCESS

ROME. To reach downtown Rome, follow I-90 (New York State Thruway) to Exit 31. Take Route 49 west in the direction of Rome.

CANAL PARK. Directions: The park is located about 10 miles east of Rome on Route 49. **Season:** Year round. **Admission:** Free. **Telephone:** None.

ERIE CANAL VILLAGE. Directions: From downtown area, follow Route 46/49 (Erie Boulevard) west. Entrance to village will be on your left, about 10 minutes from the center of Rome. **Season:** Early May through October. **Admission:** Charged. **Telephone:** (315) 336-6000.

FORT RICKEY GAME FARM. Directions: Located three miles west of Rome on Route 46/49. **Season:** Daily from late May through August. **Admission:** Charged. **Telephone:** (315) 336-1930.

FORT STANWIX NATIONAL MONUMENT. Directions: The fort is located in the center of Rome. Take Exit 31 off I-90 (New York State Thruway). Follow Route 49 west to the fort. **Season:** April 1 through December 31. **Admission:** Free. **Telephone:** (315) 336-2090.

REVERE WARE FACTORY STORE. Directions: The store is located on Railroad Street in the downtown area, 1½ blocks east of Fort Stanwix. **Season:** Year round. **Admission:** Free. Telephone: (315) 338-2223.

For lodging and restaurant suggestions, contact the Chamber of Commerce, 218 Liberty Plaza, Rome, N.Y. 13440. **Telephone:** (315) 337-1700.

The Thousand Islands Region

A castle on the Rhine? Boldt Castle is an ambitious but unfinished labor of love.

S eparating the United States from Canada, the St. Lawrence River flows seven miles wide in the Thousand Islands area. Truth to tell, there were, at last count, 1,652 bona fide islands in this part of the river. Some measure only a few square feet, while the largest is 22 miles long. They bear names like "Devil's Oven," "Just Room Enough," and "Knobby Island." Visitors flock to the region each summer to enjoy its natural attributes and its bustling resort facilities. But one problem with popular vacation spots is that they often turn out to be more touristy than some of us prefer. Seeking to address that problem, our Thousand Islands itinerary focuses on two very different towns.

The town of Alexandria Bay pulls out all the stops in the summer and closes up tight in the winter. This hub of tourism in the Thousand Islands region caters to a mix of vacationers that includes young people, families, and retirees. One of the main occupations here is just hanging out: watching and joining the endless parade of people who come to enjoy the festive atmosphere and visit the shops that line the streets. Alexandria Bay is an unpretentious town where you don't need to dress up or spend big bucks to have a good time.

The one obligatory activity is a boat trip to **Boldt Castle,** the only authentic Rhineland-style

castle in North America. George Boldt came to America in the 1860s from Prussia. He eventually became the most successful hotel magnate in the country, and his holdings included the Waldorf-Astoria in New York City. He adored his wife, Louise, and built the castle around the turn of the century as a symbol of his love for her. The heart motif is woven into the architecture and design of the six-story, 120-room edifice. The elaborate summer home was well underway when Mrs. Boldt died. Boldt ordered all work on the castle to come to a halt. Three hundred workmen left the island, and the castle was never completed.

Boldt's ill-fated summer home is located on Heart Island, and you can either get there by tour boat or rent a boat and do it yourself. Here you will wander through the ruins of an unfinished castle that has suffered the ravages of time. Efforts are underway to restore the castle, but for now, you'll need to resort to your imagination to visualize the grandeur that might have been had Louise lived. A slide show is presented in the ground floor ballroom to orient you to the family and the castle, but there are no tour guides here. You explore the grounds and the crumbling interior on your own.

Uncle Sam Boat Tours and **1000 Islands Paul Boat Line Tours** both offer regularly scheduled sightseeing cruises and ferry service directly to and from Heart Island. The direct crossing only takes about five minutes. With Uncle Sam, you can choose between a modern Mississippi-style paddle-wheeler or an original wooden tour boat dating back to the early 1900s. Almost all tours permit an unlimited stop at Boldt Castle (you just pick up a later boat when you're ready to return to the mainland). Tours range from one to five hours. On the Paul Boat Line tours, you'll travel on narrow boats that hold only 50 passengers, seating two on each side of the center aisle so that you are never more than one seat away from the side of the boat, making for good visibility as you explore the river.

If you would prefer to explore the islands independently, check out **O'Brien Boats.** Weave your way through the boats in the backyard and into the boathouse, which smells of oil and is lined with parts and marine paraphernalia. You can rent rowboats, canoes, and runabouts here. Boats range from 12 to 20 feet in length, and are powered by 3.6 to 140 horsepower Mercury motors. Fishing tackle can be rented here, too. Rentals are available by the hour, day, or week; river maps are included. You can

UNCLE SAM BOAT TOURS, INC.

Uncle Sam Boat Tours' Island Wanderer *is only one of many ways to get a closer look at Boldt Castle.*

always take yourself over to Heart Island for a look at the castle, but the staff here will also suggest other places to go — publicly owned islands where you can swim and picnic and enjoy the natural splendor.

You'll also want to allow time to explore Alexandria Bay proper, pausing at shops that catch your fancy. We treated ourselves to a "Monster Bagel" (ham, turkey, corned beef, provolone, Swiss cheese, lettuce, and tomato) and a hot "nacho bagel" at **The Stuffed Bagel.** Then, feeling truly decadent, we topped it off with a box of 1000 Island Pebbles, tiny spotted sugar confections with fruit and creme centers, which we bought at **Aunt Mary's Candystand.** Eager to work off the calories, we walked down to **Scenic View Park** to watch the almost endless procession of houseboats, motorboats, and sailboats. (We nearly jumped out of our socks as a huge freighter, the *Willow Glen*, sounded her horn.) A small footbridge leads to Casino Island, where picnic tables and grills overlook the water. There's also a small swimming beach next to the park, with some playground equipment for the kids.

Just a few miles south of Alexandria Bay, you'll come to **Wellesley Island State Park,** where you can pitch your tent and do some hiking and swimming in a lovely setting. The 2,636-acre park also includes a nine-hole golf course and boating facilities. At the **Store and Marina,** you can rent a 14-foot aluminum boat, with or without a 10 horsepower engine. Bait and tackle are available, too — everything you need to land yourself a bass, northern pike, or even a muskie.

The Minna Anthony Common Nature Center, housed in a high-ceilinged modern building, includes a nature museum with live fish, reptile, and amphibian displays; an observation beehive; and collections of mounted birds and geological specimens. Take a walk along the eight-mile network of nature trails, some winding along the edge of the St. Lawrence River, others meandering through habitats that vary from wooded wetlands to prairie vegetation. One trail is specially marked for the blind, with interpretive signs in braille and raised letters that point out sounds to listen for, scents to identify, and minerals to touch.

In the winter you can cross-country ski along the center's seven miles of groomed trails. Lessons are available on Saturdays, and you can either rent equipment or bring your own. The center also keeps a supply of snowshoes on hand, which you're wel-

We nearly jumped out of our socks as a huge freighter, the Willow Glen, *sounded her horn.*

come to try out. There's a large stone fireplace in the middle of the exhibit area, and a fire is always crackling on a nippy day. Bring along a picnic and purchase cocoa, soup, and coffee on the spot.

Here on Wellesley Island, you're only minutes away from Canada. Continuing across the next span of the Thousand Islands Bridge, you'll find yourself on Hill Island, Ontario. You'll have to go through customs, so be sure to bring along a driver's license or other form of identification. Tell the immigration agent you're heading for the **1000 Islands Skydeck,** just a few hundred yards distant. You'll travel upward in an express elevator, which takes only 40 seconds to reach the glass-enclosed deck at the 320-foot level. On a clear day, the field of visibility is about 40 miles. You'll look out over a panorama of evergreen islands, with narrow channels winding among them. For an even better view, climb the stairs to the open-air upper deck. Not high enough? Continue on up to the crow's-nest.

On a clear day, you'll look out over a panorama of evergreen islands, with narrow channels winding among them.

At the base of the skydeck, there's a restaurant for lunch or snacks. There is also a separate exhibit center. In the summer of 1985, this building housed Science Circus, a traveling show put on by the Ontario Science Centre. The show includes over 50 participatory exhibits designed to illuminate the world of science. Play a probability game. Make sand pictures with the compound pendulum. Operate a robot. The Science Circus was operating at the skydeck on a pilot basis, but if all goes well it is expected to make regular summer stays here on Hill Island. Just be certain to call ahead.

Continue on to the town of Clayton, which is quiet and unspoiled, the perfect place to head if you want to visit the famous Thousand Islands region but don't feel up for the commercialism and jazzy atmosphere of Alexandria Bay. For some, Clayton is dull in comparison to its more spirited neighbor. For others, it offers a serenity and simplicity that make it the hands-down favorite.

Begin your day at **Thousand Islands Shipyard Museum,** right on the waterfront in Clayton's French Creek Bay. The museum presents the history of freshwater boating, an important enterprise in a part of the world where people's lives were (and still are, in many ways) entwined with the sea. The collection includes about 150 boats, 200 outboard and inboard engines, and over 12,000 artifacts. Many of the boats are of local origin. There are simple cedar skiffs and high-speed racers, birchbark canoes and elegant launches. As you explore the yards and

buildings, you'll hear hammers banging and smell the strong scent of varnish. This is not a static museum, but a place where boats are constantly being restored or repaired.

The motor launch Restless, *circa 1890, with a high-spirited boating party on board.*

The displays give the visitor a strong feeling of how boats reflect the character of the people who use them. A mannequin representing Dr. Homer L. Dodge, renowned as the American dean of whitewater canoeing, poses contentedly in his sail-rigged Grumman aluminum canoe, next to a placard bearing a Dodge quote: "When I'm happiest after a nice day of sailing or paddling, or perhaps handling some rapids successfully — then after a good campfire and a meal I roll out in a sleeping bag and sleep under the stars." Turn-of-the-century launches, with polished decks and awnings above, create a mental image of the people who skimmed the water on the likes of the *Minnie, Anita,* and *Pastime.* Other artifacts testify to the inventiveness of boat builders. Take the 1915-vintage dispro (disappearing propeller), also called the "stump jumper," which was used for shallow-water touring and fishing. The guide could pull the propeller up into the hull through a hole in the floor when the going got rough.

Outside, a young visitor pulls hard on the wheel in an old lobster boat that's meant for play. "There's a whale at one o'clock!" he screams, ringing a bell enthusiastically. Kids also enjoy historic cruises on the *Narra Mattah,* a 1902 ELCO glass cabin cruiser that makes regularly scheduled tours of the islands, departing from the museum's main dock. A free ride is included in the museum's admission price.

For a look at some other aspects of Clayton's

Outside a young visitor pulls hard on the wheel in an old lobster boat that's meant exclusively for play.

heritage, try the **Thousand Islands Museum.** Here you can step inside a group of re-created building façades for a taste of 19th-century Clayton. In Clayton High School, kids were using a text called *The Progressive Road to Reading.* The pharmacy peddles souvenirs popular at the turn of the century, like a blue atomizer and a red glass canoe that each say "1000 Islands." The brick, clapboard, and shingled façades also open onto the hotel lobby, the fire department, the train office, and the Locklin Millinery, where one could purchase beribboned headgear and graceful parasols. The downstairs part of the museum houses an excellent collection of decoys. And be sure to take a look at the ingenious duck boat with the mechanically reversing oars.

If you admire fine handwork, you'll want to stop by at the **Thousand Islands Craft School and Textile Museum,** which is housed in one of the oldest houses in Clayton. Special exhibits are arranged each season — we saw a show devoted to fine lace. The early and modern pieces, including lace gloves, collars, handkerchiefs, shawls, and cuffs, were attractively displayed in a homey setting that incorporated a few plants along with books, patterns, and equipment used to make the lace. In the cheerful stenciled hallway with the orange floor, you can purchase handcrafted items ranging from tinsel and theorem paintings to more utilitarian pieces like pottery bowls and handwoven placemats. We were enchanted by a painting under glass of St. George reluctantly stabbing a slightly silly-looking dragon.

Be sure to take a look at the ingenious duck boat with the mechanically reversing oars.

The craft school offers a series of workshops and classes lasting from one evening to two weeks. Weekend workshops begin Friday evening and run all day Saturday and Sunday. Evening workshops run three consecutive nights. The school prides itself on the quality and experience of its instructors, many of whom are nationally known for their work. The general subject areas covered in the courses are: Weaving and Basketry, Metals and Stones, Drawing and Painting, Pottery, Carving, Lace and Embroidery, Early American Decoration, Quilting, and Painting and Printing on Fabric. Specialized workshops and classes are offered in each category. Write ahead for a schedule.

Like Alexandria Bay, Clayton offers boat trips to the famous islands themselves. Sign on for a narrated **Gray Line of the 1000 Islands** tour. Double-decker modern aluminum boats wend their way in and out of the channels, past islands large and small. You'll see elegant island estates, and you may well get a close-up view of a mammoth freighter en route from the Midwest to some distant foreign port. All trips stop at Heart Island, where you can get off and visit **Boldt Castle**. (See description on pages 107-108.) There is a snack bar aboard and a full-service cocktail bar opens up on the sunset cruise.

If you head home by driving south from Clayton, stop off at the **Thousand Islands Apiaries.** The small retail store contains a glass demonstration hive where you can watch bees at work: cleaning the hive, gathering food, and caring for the young. Much of the honey sold here is produced by area beekeepers, but there are a couple of hives out back, and the person tending shop will gladly show them to you if you ask. Be sure to take home a jar of liquid honey, honey comb, or honey cream, a smooth, crystallized spread that comes in three flavors — plain, cinnamon, or maple-flavored.

Your feet will be happy to learn that you can take an express elevator to the top of the 1000 Islands Skydeck.

BRIGDENS, LTD./1000 ISLANDS SKYDECK

ACCESS

ALEXANDRIA BAY. To reach Alexandria Bay, follow I-81 north to Exit 50A. Take Route 12 into Alexandria Bay.

BOLDT CASTLE. Directions: Located on Heart Island; accessible from Alexandria Bay by boat. **Season:** Mid-May through mid-October. **Admission:** Charged. **Telephone:** (315) 482-2501.

UNCLE SAM BOAT TOURS. Directions: Boats depart from dock at base of James Street in Alexandria Bay. **Season:** Mid-May through mid-October. **Admission:** Charged. **Telephone:** (315) 482-2611 or (315) 482-9611.

1000 ISLANDS PAUL BOAT LINE TOURS. Directions: Boats depart near the base of Church Street in Alexandria Bay. **Season:** Mid-May through mid-October. **Admission:** Charged. **Telephone:** (315) 482-9511 or (315) 482-9351.

O'BRIEN BOATS. Directions: Located on Walton Street in Alexandria Bay. **Season:** April through October. **Admission:** Rental fees. **Telephone:** (315) 482-9548.

THE STUFFED BAGEL. Directions: Located at 23 Market Street in Alexandria Bay. **Season:** June through September. **Admission:** Free. **Telephone:** None.

AUNT MARY'S CANDYSTAND. Directions: Located on James Street in Alexandria Bay. **Season:** June through September. **Admission:** Free. **Telephone:** None.

SCENIC VIEW PARK. Directions: Across the street from the parking area for Paul Boat Line Tours. **Season:** Year round. **Admission:** Free. **Telephone:** None.

WELLESLEY ISLAND STATE PARK. Directions: The entrance to the park is reached by following Route 12 to the Thousand Islands International Bridge, between Alexandria Bay and Clayton. **Season:** Year round. **Admission:** Charged. **Telephone:** (315) 482-2722.

STORE AND MARINA. Directions: Located within the state park. **Season:** May through September. **Admission:** Boat rental fees. **Telephone:** (315) 482-3314.

MINNA ANTHONY COMMON NATURE CENTER. Directions: Located in the state park. **Season:** Year round. **Admission:** Free. **Telephone:** (315) 482-2479.

1000 ISLANDS SKYDECK. Directions: Located on Hill Island, Ontario, Canada, between the spans of the Thousand Islands International Bridge. Cross to Wellesley Island and continue across to Hill Island. **Season:** May through October. **Admission:** Charged. **Telephone:** (613) 659-2335.

CLAYTON. To reach Clayton, follow I-81 to Exit 47. Follow signs into Clayton via Route 12.

THOUSAND ISLANDS SHIPYARD MUSEUM. Directions: The museum is located at 750 Mary Street in Clayton. Follow signs from Route 12. **Season:** Mid-May to mid-October. **Admission:** Charged. **Telephone:** (315) 686-4104.

THOUSAND ISLANDS MUSEUM. Directions: Located at 403 Riverside Drive in Clayton, in the Old Town Hall. **Season:** Memorial Day to Labor Day. **Admission:** Charged. **Telephone:** (315) 686-5794.

THOUSAND ISLANDS CRAFT SCHOOL AND TEXTILE MUSEUM. Directions: Located at 314 John Street in Clayton. **Season:** Museum is open late March through October. Craft school operates from mid-June to mid-September. **Admission:** Donations accepted. **Telephone:** (315) 686-4123.

GRAY LINE OF THE 1000 ISLANDS. Directions: Boats depart from 604 Riverside Drive in Clayton. **Season:** May 15 through October 15. **Admission:** Charged. **Telephone:** (315) 686-3511.

THOUSAND ISLANDS APIARIES. Directions: Located on Route 12E, halfway between Clayton and Cape Vincent. **Season:** Mid-June through mid-September. **Admission:** Free. **Telephone:** (315) 654-2741.

For lodging and restaurant suggestions, contact the Clayton Chamber of Commerce at Riverside Drive, Clayton, N.Y. 13624. **Telephone:** (315) 686-3771.

Seneca Falls

A rural farming community up until the 1830s, Seneca Falls experienced great change during the Industrial Revolution. Mills and other manufacturing concerns sprouted up alongside the Seneca River, leashing the power of its five natural falls and forever changing the place of women in the community. For the first time, women had the option of working for wages instead of simply working in the home. However they came by their wages, they soon learned that their husbands were entitled to everything they earned, and that they couldn't own property, even if they were single and had cash of their own from their work. Nor could they inherit their husbands' estates or serve as legal guardians of their own children. They couldn't even work to change these laws, since it was considered improper for them to speak in public and because they couldn't vote.

The Great Western Turnpike, a major transportation route, became the main street of Seneca Falls before 1800. By 1828, the community was linked to the Erie Canal system, and by 1841 the railroad passed through town. Because of its position as a transportation hub, many reformers, radicals, pioneers, and dreamers also passed through, leaving behind their influence and creating an atmosphere conducive to social change.

Elizabeth Cady Stanton moved to Seneca Falls from Boston in 1847. Discontented with the narrow limits of her life in the isolated community, she shared her frustrations with other local women. Within a year, the group organized the first Wom-

Activist or no, Elizabeth Cady Stanton had her hands full raising seven children in this Seneca Falls home.

Elizabeth Cady Stanton's Declaration of Sentiments declared "all men and women are created equal."

en's Rights Convention, in the Wesleyan Chapel right here in Seneca Falls. Several days later she and her four fellow organizers met again to draft their grievances into a Declaration of Sentiments modeled after the Declaration of Independence. The statement declared "all men and women are created equal" and demanded the right to vote in addition to 17 other rights. The story of the women's rights movement is the theme of the **Women's Rights National Historical Park,** established in 1980.

The park is still very much in the developmental stages, but there are two buildings currently open to visitors. Begin at the visitor center, where there are interpretive exhibits including two slide shows — one focusing on the history of the women's movement and the other on the development of the park. A park ranger will give you a 15-minute guided tour of the photos and documents in the center. You'll hear about the major restrictions experienced by Elizabeth Cady Stanton and her contemporaries, but you'll also hear about lesser-known ways in which women were limited. Even the fashions of the day worked against them. Women might have earned the label "the weaker sex" partly because they wore up to 15 petticoats at a time, weighing as much as 25 pounds. With corsets designed to engineer their waists into 12-inch wonders, their lungs were squooshed against their other innards, greatly reducing endurance! When Amelia Bloomer, who supported dress reform, published patterns for a pantaloon-and-tunic outfit (nicknamed "bloomers") in her newspaper, *The Lilly*, circulation jumped from 500 to 4,000 copies per month. Yet women were so mocked when they wore the more comfortable garments that many went back to conventional clothing: "We put on the dress for greater freedom," remarked Cady Stanton, referring to the bloomer sets, "but what is physical freedom compared with mental bondage?"

Women wore up to 15 petticoats at a time, weighing as much as 25 pounds.

From the visitor center, your guide will direct you to the meticulously restored Elizabeth Cady Stanton House. When we say meticulous, we mean it. The building was stripped to its frame and the roof of the south wing had to be lowered from two to one and a half stories. Nothing was left to chance. Before reconstructing the gardens and plantings, an agricultural archeologist was hired to dig a trench and make microscopic studies of soil samples in order to determine pollen species dating back to Stanton's time. Details within the house illuminate the lifestyle of the mid-19th century.

Park ranger Anne Swiatek leads a bicycle tour of historic sites in the Women's Rights National Historical Park.

Painted and shellacked floorcloths, for example, were used instead of carpeting, because carpets were considered an agent of disease contagion. During the restoration, up to 15 layers of wallpaper had to be removed and studied in order to come up with an authentic design.

The more interest you show, the more thoroughly your guide will delve into Stanton family history. Elizabeth had seven kids, and we heard about the time two of the older boys set a younger brother afloat on a raft. This stunt incurred their mother's wrath, but it didn't stop them from tying the poor kid to a chimney a few days later.

The park also offers several special events during the summer months, including regularly scheduled walking tours of Seneca Falls and a series of lunchtime lectures on subjects like Dress Reform and Women and Abolition. There are also free narrated boat tours along the barge canal and past the Seneca Knitting Mill, which is still in operation today. Because the park is still growing and changing, it is important to call ahead for an update on all events.

Just down the street from the visitor center, you can visit the **National Women's Hall of Fame,** the only national organization in the country whose goal is "to honor in perpetuity those women, citizens of the United States of America, whose contributions to the arts, athletics, business, education, government, humanitarianism, philanthropy, and science, have been of the greatest value for the development of their country." A 10-minute slide show recaps highlights of the development of the women's rights movement in 19th-century Seneca Falls (if you've already seen the presentation at the National Historic Park, you may want to skip this one). In the main exhibit hall, displays and photographs showcase the achievements of women as varied as abolitionist Harriet Tubman and painter Mary Cassatt, anthropologist Margaret Mead and medical researcher Florence Sabin.

Each of the women honored is represented by a photograph and a placard describing her achievements. Some of them are also accompanied by a telephone-like device. Pick up the receiver and listen as Marian Anderson, who traveled from childhood poverty in Philadelphia to the stage of the Metropolitan Opera House, sings "He's Got the Whole World in His Hands." Eleanor Roosevelt, who worked tirelessly on behalf of the poor, the blacks, and the unemployed, reflects on her relationship with her famous husband: "He knew that life would be very uninteresting to me if I didn't feel I was doing something useful." She goes on to explain that FDR used her as a check, to counterbalance the information and impressions he garnered from official sources.

If you plan to spend the night in Seneca Falls and are game for a place that's out of the ordinary, try **The Gould Hotel.** Two earlier hotels occupied this site before the present one was built by Norman Gould of Goulds Pumps in 1920; both previous hotels were destroyed by fire. The Gould offered furnished apartments, a new concept in 1920s hotel management. Today it continues to offer seven of these apartments to the public on a nightly basis. For the price of a room at a major motel chain, we spent the night in a suite consisting of a huge, attractively furnished living room, a large bedroom with spacious bathroom, and a full-fledged modern kitchen. We were within easy walking distance of both the Women's Hall of Fame and the National Historic Site. There isn't much going on at night in Seneca Falls, but the attractive, Victorian-era bar at The Gould is a pleasant place to while away the evening. There is also a handsome walnut-col-

GENEVA HISTORICAL SOCIETY

Influential farmer Robert Swan owned Rose Hill, a Greek revival mansion overlooking Seneca Lake.

umned dining room where you can enjoy a leisurely lunch or dinner or Sunday brunch.

An elegant 19th-century country estate crowned with a Greek revival mansion, **Rose Hill,** in nearby Geneva, stands in stark contrast to the Stanton house in Seneca Falls. An important technique in farming technology was developed at Rose Hill (considered one of the most innovative farms in the state in its day) by owner Robert Swan, who installed the first large-scale drainage system, using ceramic-tile pipes to drain marshy land. He was rewarded with bountiful crops, and soon his technique was adopted by many other farmers.

A visit to Rose Hill begins with a brief orientation film describing the house and the people who lived in it. Then you'll take a 40-minute guided tour through the mansion. But first pause for a moment beneath the massive central portico, supported by six Ionic columns, to enjoy the view of Seneca Lake. Inside, Rose Hill boasts graceful wood and plaster moldings, like the grapevine design you'll see on the columns leading to the back parlor with its view of the wheatfields. The house is furnished in Empire style, and the paint colors, wallpapers, and textiles used are typical of the period. In the front parlor, notice the rosewood carving on the couches. There's a blue-and-gold wallpaper border around the top of the parlor bedroom that looks almost like a valance. The kitchen has pumpkin-colored paint on the walls, to pick up the color of the hearth bricks. The kitchen floor was bleached, salted, and scrubbed to ensure cleanliness.

Throughout the tour, your guide will point out unusual accessories and pieces of furniture — like the pigeon-hole desk with extra broad writing surface to accommodate cumbersome law ledgers, the painted pie safe with star-patterned tin insets, the hand-painted playing cards and mother-of-pearl playing chips, and the black-and-white Staffordshire footbath.

If you are intrigued by 19th-century architecture, you will want to continue into the center of Geneva. Stop in at the **Geneva Historical Society Museum,** which contains period rooms and displays related to the history of Geneva. Pick up a walking tour leaflet (often available at Rose Hill also), and take a self-guided tour of South Main Street. More than two dozen points of interest are noted, ranging from renovated Federal-style row houses to an apartment building that used to house

Robert Swan installed the first large-scale drainage system, using ceramic-tile pipes to drain marshy land.

The kitchen floor was bleached, salted, and scrubbed to ensure cleanliness.

The Hygienic Institute (for the "scientific treatment of disease and ailments"), from the Gothic Revival-style Trinity Church to the high Victorian Gothic "Dove House," with its heavy gable trim. The tour also includes the home of Mrs. Ricord's Female Seminary (1830s) and the Richardsonian-Romanesque Collins Music Hall, with its round arches and rough stone exterior. By the time you've completed the loop, you'll have a real sense of the flavor of life in Geneva over a hundred years ago.

ACCESS

SENECA FALLS. To reach Seneca Falls, follow I-90 (New York State Thruway) to Exit 41. Continue by going south on Route 414, then east on Route 5/20.

WOMEN'S RIGHTS NATIONAL HISTORICAL PARK. Directions: The visitor center is located at 116 Fall Street in downtown Seneca Falls. You will receive a map directing you to other sites included in the park. **Season:** Year round. **Admission:** Free. **Telephone:** (315) 568-2991.

NATIONAL WOMEN'S HALL OF FAME. Directions: Located at 76 Fall Street in downtown Seneca Falls. **Season:** Year round. **Admission:** Charged. **Telephone:** (315) 568-8060.

THE GOULD HOTEL. Directions: Located on Fall Street in downtown Seneca Falls. **Season:** Year round. **Admission:** Free. **Telephone:** (315) 568-5801.

ROSE HILL. Directions: From I-90 (New York State Thruway), take Exit 41. Travel south on Route 414; then west on Route 5/20. Turn left on Route 96A and continue one mile to Rose Hill. **Season:** May through October. **Admission:** Charged. **Telephone:** (315) 789-3848.

GENEVA HISTORICAL SOCIETY MUSEUM. Directions: Follow I-90 (New York State Thruway) to Exit 42. Take Route 14 south to Geneva. (From Rose Hill, follow Route 96A to Route 14.) Museum is on Route 14 (South Main Street). **Season:** Year round. **Admission:** Donations accepted. **Telephone:** (315) 789-5151.

For lodging and restaurant suggestions, contact the Seneca Chamber of Commerce, 2022 Seneca Falls Waterloo Road, P.O. Box 294, Seneca Falls, N.Y. 14456. **Telephone:** (315) 789-1776.

Along Cayuga Lake

OFFICE OF PARKS, RECREATION & HISTORIC PRESERVATION

The first day of trout season attracts hopeful anglers to the Lower Falls in Taughannock Falls State Park.

S pend a peaceful, unhurried day or two exploring the western shore of Cayuga, largest of the Finger Lakes. Combine some hiking, camping, and swimming with stops at family businesses that welcome visitors. If you like to meet local people in your travels, or if you enjoy learning about unusual lifestyles, a trip to Cayuga country fits the bill perfectly. The pastoral scenery provides the perfect backdrop for some low-key, laid-back exploring.

Begin with a visit to the **Misty Meadow Hog Farm,** where Ann and Fred Sepe and their family raise over 1,000 pigs a year. This is truly a family business. A grandmother tends the small gift shop, and whichever of the five Sepe kids happen to be home help out with the work. The Sepes have been here 10 years, and you get the feeling they're going to stay put. A family member will take you on a 45-minute tour, beginning in the farrowing barn where the pigs are born.

Piglets weigh about three pounds at birth and grow to 220 pounds in less than six months. You'll learn that they eat grain and soybeans and that the conversion factor is about three to one, meaning that it takes about 660 pounds of feed to create 220

Priscilla Sepe holds one of the newest members of the family at Misty Meadow Hog Farm.

pounds of pig. Pigs are very self-sufficient animals. As soon as they're born they stand up and start nursing. They stay in the farrowing pens about two weeks. After that two mother pigs are moved in together with their litters, and in no time at all their smells get mixed up and the piglets nurse from one or the other indiscriminately.

When they're four weeks old, the youngsters are moved into the nursery, the most popular stop on the tour. Ann Sepe, our guide, handed each willing adult a squirming piglet to hold. Kids get to sort of hold them (together with their parents, to avoid accidental dropping). You think kittens and puppies are appealing? Just try cuddling a squealing pink piglet! You'll never stereotype pigs as dirty, ugly beasts again. And while we're at it, when you *do* see dirty pigs it's usually for a good reason. We learned that they have a high body temperature but no sweat glands, which means that they like to get wet in order to cool off.

From the nursery, you'll go into the large barn, then past the breeding pens and on to the finishing barn, where hogs are grown to market size. You'll get to feed middling-size pigs (400- to 500-pound range) and you'll meet about 70 sows and six boars, some of whom weigh in close to 1,000 pounds. You'll learn that pigs continue to grow all their lives. "The record is about 1,800 pounds," Ann explains, "and when they get up near that size they look just like little Volkswagen bugs." You'll hear about a lot of other important pig lore, too. Pigskin, for example, is used in skin grafts, and insulin was first synthesized from pigs.

When the tour is over, head for the spacious lunch pavilion overlooking the cornfields and Lake Cayuga beyond. Stuff yourself on woodsmoked slices of pork barbecue, slathered with Ann's own sauce. Hot dogs, hamburgers, and sausage sandwiches are available, too. It's strictly self-service and moderately priced. Then finish up with a slab of homemade blackberry pie à la mode. While we ate, Ann spoke with enthusiasm about the area she lives in. "Swine, wine, and dine on Route 89," she laughed, "that's how I like to put it."

Ann sent us packing along the "Cayuga Wine Trail," which extends 40 miles, north to south, along the western shore of Cayuga Lake. There are five wineries in all, and you can visit just one or the whole handful. We chose two, and found them different enough from each other to think that we could have happily explored all five.

We stopped at **Plane's Cayuga Vineyard,** a 195-acre spread that slopes upward away from the lake. Former college president Robert Plane is the winemaker; his wife Mary is vineyard manager. They raise French hybrids and vinifera on 40 of their acres, selling off surplus grapes to other wine producers. During the fall harvest (call ahead to check exact dates), they also have juice and grapes available for home winemakers. The vineyard strives to produce wines "that show true varietal character." Plane's produces a Chardonnay, Cayuga White, a Chancellor, a Ravat Vignoles, and a Riesling.

The winery is housed in a cavernous barn that opens onto the vineyard. The tasting area includes an open balcony with a lovely view of the lake and vineyards; here you can sample the wines and make purchases. There is also a deli counter where you can put together a picnic of cheese, pâté, rolls, and fresh fruit to eat on the grounds. The loft area serves as an art gallery, an airy showplace for regional handcrafts. There are hand-painted scarves and handmade paper objects, stained glass kaleidoscopes and hand-woven rag rugs.

The lower level of the barn serves as the wine cellar. It holds the stainless steel tanks and oak barrels used for fermenting and storing the wines. The informal tours take 10 to 15 minutes. You'll learn that some of the grapes are machine picked while others are harvested by hand. They are then fed through the press and tubed into the cellar. In the fermentation tanks, the natural sugar in the grapes is converted to alcohol. The fermentation process usually takes about a month, and is followed by a month or two of "settling." You'll see the sterile bottling room where the bottles, fed in by hand, are filled and corked. Outside the bottling room, they are labeled and "crimped" (the tops put on).

A few miles south of here, you'll come to **Lucas Vineyards,** another family-owned and operated estate winery. Ruth Lucas tends the winery and vineyards full time, while her husband Bill divides his time between the vineyard and his job as a tugboat pilot in New York Harbor. The Lucases moved from New York City to this former dairy farm in Interlaken in 1974. They planted their first grapes in 1975 and harvested their first crop in 1977, which they sold to neighboring wineries. In 1980 they held back 10 tons of grapes for the first bottling under their own label. Today they welcome visitors to their winery, tasting room, and wine shop. During harvest time they also sell juice, grapes, and

Bill Lucas divides his time between the vineyard and his job as a tugboat pilot in New York Harbor.

At Cornell Plantations, you can learn a lot about the local environment. You may even run into some students doing the very same thing.

The blue-gray layer of limestone that forms the bottom of the gorge is made up of the skeletons of billions of ancient sea creatures.

winemaking supplies. They're also happy to explain how they grow their grapes and make their wine.

Continuing south, you'll come to **Taughannock Falls State Park.** The 738-acre park includes 76 campsites, 16 cabins, boat launching ramps, an attractive swimming lake with a beach and bathhouse, picnic tables and fireplaces. There is also a lovely playground with imaginative wooden towers and platforms to climb on, set in a shady grove near the edge of the lake. The park includes one mile of shoreline, providing plenty of opportunity for fishing in Taughannock Creek and Cayuga Lake. Cross-country skiing and ice skating are prime winter activities.

Whether you spend a few hours or a few days here, you'll want to hike up the Taughannock Falls Gorge Trail. As recently as a mere 10,000 years ago the falls cascaded right into Cayuga Lake. But time and nature have moved the falls nearly a mile away from the shoreline. At the bottom of the trail you can pick up a guide to 14 points of interest corresponding to numbered posts. As you ascend the trail, you'll notice the blue-gray layer of limestone that forms the bottom of the gorge. It is made up of the compressed, disintegrated skeletons of billions of ancient sea creatures.

After about half an hour of hiking, you'll be rewarded with a view of 215-foot Taughannock Falls, the highest straight-drop waterfall in the United States (higher even than Niagara Falls). The stone walls on either side soar skyward nearly 400 feet, and the "plunge pool" at the base is over 30 feet deep. Yet the falls itself is a narrow, delicate stream of water, cascading into the gorge below.

Continuing south, you'll come to Ithaca. Here you can visit the **Cornell Plantations.** The plantations encompass 2,800 acres and include formal gardens, an arboretum, and a network of nature trails that wind through gorges, ponds, streams, and forests. You'll see alpine and wetland plants and specialty gardens that focus on herbs, wildflowers, poisonous plants, peonies, vegetables, and flowers for cutting and drying. Detailed leaflets are found in wooden boxes near each garden. The plantations offer an ideal place for walking or jogging, or for just sitting peacefully and enjoying the good things that grow all around.

ACCESS

CAYUGA LAKE. To reach the Cayuga Lake area, follow I-90 (New York State Thruway) to Exit 41; take Route 318 east to Route 89. Continue south on Route 89, which borders the lake.

MISTY MEADOW HOG FARM. Directions: Located on Vineyard Road in Romulus, off Route 89. Follow signs from Route 89. **Season:** Late June through mid-September. **Admission:** Charged. **Telephone:** (315) 549-8839, or (607) 869-9243.

PLANE'S CAYUGA VINEYARD. Directions: Located on Route 89 in Ovid. **Season:** Daily (afternoons only) from Memorial Day through Labor Day; weekends (afternoons only) during off-season. **Admission:** Tours are free. Small charge for tasting, but can be applied to wine purchase. **Telephone:** (607) 869-5158.

LUCAS VINEYARDS. Directions: Located just north of Interlaken on Route 89. **Season:** Daily in July and August. Weekends from Memorial Day through June and September through October. **Admission:** Free. **Telephone:** (607) 532-4825.

TAUGHANNOCK FALLS STATE PARK. Directions: Located on Route 89 near Trumansburg. **Season:** Year round; camping from March 31 to mid-October. **Admission:** Charged; no parking fees in winter. **Telephone:** (607) 387-6739.

CORNELL PLANTATIONS. Directions: From Route 13 in Ithaca, take Route 79 east for 1.2 miles, then bear left on Route 366. Continue l.l miles to the left-hand intersection onto Judd Falls Road. Turn left. Take the first right after the stop sign. Follow signs. **Season:** Year round. **Admission:** Free. **Telephone:** (607) 256-3020.

For lodging and restaurant suggestions, contact the Tomkins County Chamber of Commerce, 122 West Court Street, Ithaca, N.Y. 14853. **Telephone:** (607) 273-7080. For a copy of the Cayuga Wine Trail brochure, write to Cayuga Wine Trail, R.D. 2, Box 273, Ovid, N.Y. 14521.

Watkins Glen

C onveniently situated in the center of the Finger Lakes district, Watkins Glen is a lively vacation spot, with plenty of shops to explore and places to eat. But the real attractions here are the natural ones: Seneca Lake and a spectacular gorge that traces its origins back 10,000 years to the end of the last Ice Age. For well over a century, visitors have been attracted to the breathtaking chasm, which today forms the heart of **Watkins Glen State Park.** Traveling south from Canada, great continental glaciers ripped a huge gash in an ancient river valley, creating 38-mile-long Seneca Lake, one of the deepest bodies of water in the United States. Since that time, Glen Creek has poured down the glacially steepened valleyside, methodically carving out the gorge in a process that continues to this day.

The best way to experience the drama and beauty of the glen is to hike the gorge trail. The trail is 1½ miles long and has over 800 stone steps. Starting at the main entrance to the park, it is an uphill trek. Some visitors prefer to take a shuttle bus from the main entrance to the upper entrance, just hiking down the trail instead of undertaking the round trip on foot. It is not a difficult walk; however, the footing can get slippery, so do wear suitable footgear. While the park itself remains open in the winter for

Rainbow Falls, one of the many natural wonders in the gorge at Watkins Glen.

hiking, cross-country skiing, and snowmobiling, the gorge trail is closed.

Numbered markers along the trail refer to entries in a printed leaflet that introduces important features of the gorge. The chasm itself extends two miles into the mountainside; it is characterized by a series of grottos, caves, and cataracts, and by its 19 waterfalls, bearing names like Rainbow, Diamond, and Pluto. You'll pass through tunnels hand-cut in the rock, and under and over bridges. There are places too where you actually walk *behind* the falls. In the high "cathedral" area, you'll notice a slab of stone with a rippled surface. When you stand on it, you are standing on the floor of an ancient sea. Hundreds of millions of years ago, those ripples were ripples on a sandy underwater floor.

The park contains about 300 campsites along with many picnic areas and hiking trails. There's a 50-meter swimming pool and a children's pool, too. If you decide to spend the night in the area, you'll want to treat yourself to a performance of **Timespell.** Twice each evening in the warm-weather months, this 45-minute sound and light show breathes life and meaning into the history of the gorge.

As dusk settles, visitors crowd into the courtyard near the main entrance to the park. Some sip on wine coolers (made from New York State wines, of course), while others make a quick supper of the nachos and sandwiches sold at the refreshment stand. There is a festive, expectant feeling in the air. As darkness falls, a voice over a loudspeaker announces the beginning of the show, and we gather behind our guide to make our way up the beginning of the gorge. We feel as though we are on a nocturnal pilgrimage as we pass through a cold, damp tunnel and over a stone bridge.

As we stand at the edge of the gorge, awed by its starkness and enormity, we hear haunting music. A narrator's voice intrudes on the darkness, and we suddenly find ourselves pulled millions of years back in time. "There have been storms at sea here," the voice intones, "and vast stirrings of the earth...." The glen is a window on the past, and the story of its formation is brought to life as bright lights illuminate its sheer stone faces and rocky crags.

Using laser images, panoramic sound, and some splashy special effects, Timespell feeds our imaginations, conjuring visions of howling winds and thunderous volcanoes. As we stand in the dark, blue and white lights flash around us, and we hear a rush of wind and the sounds of an enormous mass

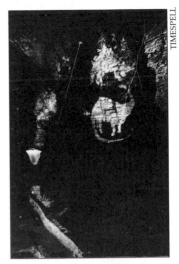

TIMESPELL

Timespell uses laser images and special effects to take you on a little history lesson, through several million years.

Hundreds of millions of years ago, these ripples in the rock were a sandy underwater floor.

Blue and white lights flash around us, and we hear a rush of wind and the sounds of an enormous, moving mass of ice.

of ice plowing southward, destroying everything in its path. We learn of a time when this part of our country was made up of mountains as high as the Himalayas — all of them under the sea. Slides of primordial seafish and worms are projected on the rocky face of the chasm. With the waterfall rushing in the background, we learn of dragonflies with three-foot wingspans and hear the roar of a prehistoric beast. When the story moves on to the Seneca Indians, who walked the gorge a mere few hundred years ago, we hear the muted beat of drums and listen to the tale of the soul gatherer. By the time we hear about a railroad line that threatened to charge extra for ladies wearing more than 20 petticoats, we feel as though we are in the present. Music fills the gorge as the show concludes and we make our way back down the stone steps with lots to think about.

As mentioned earlier, the town of Watkins Glen links the gorge with Seneca Lake. **Captain Bill's Seneca Lake Cruises** are a good way to explore the latter. The diesel-powered *Stroller IV* and other boats make a 10-mile loop around the lake, and the crew explains points of interest over the public-address system. You'll learn, for example, about the International Salt Company, which is only fitting since there are major salt mines in the area. Cruises depart at regular intervals throughout the day and early evening and take about one hour. The boats are glass enclosed, so don't worry about the weather. Back at the dock, treat yourself to a round of golf at Captain Bill's miniature golf course.

Our next stop is one that you'll either love or hate. Do you like cars, really fast ones? Then head out to the **Watkins Glen International Race Track,** which hosts seven weekends of road racing each summer. Events change each weekend, but you might see GTO and GTU sports cars compete in a three-hour duel on the 2.4-mile course, or you could watch stock cars thunder around the longer 3.377-mile circuit. For a complete racing weekend, there's even a family camping area for RVs, vans, and tents where you can watch races from the woods. Fireworks and music liven up evenings at the track.

From Watkins Glen, we suggest a sidetrip to nearby Hammondsport, with its cluster of wineries. At the **Taylor Great Western — Gold Seal Winery Visitor Center** you can take an hour-long tour that focuses on the history and techniques of winemaking. Some wines are still aged in wooden casks that have been in use for over a century. You'll visit stone cellars built into a hillside and see vintners and

From the starter's gun to the checkered flag, you'll catch all the excitement of professional auto racing at Watkins Glen International Race Track.

cellarmen at work. In the visitor center, take a seat in the unusual auditorium (constructed inside a redwood tank that once held 35,000 gallons of wine) and watch a presentation on wine production. After your tour, you'll have an opportunity to sample the wines that are made right here.

If you are passing through on a weekend, you might want to spend the evening here at Taylor Park. Tours are offered only in the daytime, but free concerts are presented each Friday evening from early July through mid-August. Bring along your own lawn chair or blanket and listen to music that covers the spectrum from folk to bluegrass, big band to symphony orchestra. When it rains the action moves indoors at a nearby school. Day and night, there's plenty to do in the Watkins Glen area.

Take a seat in the auditorium (constructed inside a redwood tank that once held 35,000 gallons of wine).

ACCESS

WATKINS GLEN. Follow Route 17 west to Route 14; travel north on Route 14 into Watkins Glen.

WATKINS GLEN STATE PARK. Directions: The main entrance is located on Route 14 (Franklin Street) in the town of Watkins Glen. **Season:** Year round; camping from mid-May to Columbus Day. **Admission:** Fees charged. **Telephone:** (607) 387-7081.

TIMESPELL. Directions: Originates at main entrance to Watkins Glen State Park. Purchase tickets here. **Season:** May through October. **Admission:** Charged. **Telephone:** (607) 535-4960.

CAPTAIN BILL'S SENECA LAKE CRUISES. Directions: Dock and ticket office are located at the foot of Franklin Street (Route 14) in Watkins Glen. **Season:** Mid-May through mid-October. **Admission:** Charged. **Telephone:** (607) 535-4541.

WATKINS GLEN INTERNATIONAL RACE TRACK. Directions: Follow Montour-Townsend Road out of the center of town in Watkins Glen; follow signs to track. **Season:** Late June through mid-October. **Admission:** Charged. **Telephone:** (607) 535-2406.

TAYLOR GREAT WESTERN — GOLD SEAL WINERY VISITOR CENTER. Directions: Follow Route 17 to Exit 38 at Bath. From Bath take Route 54 north for about five miles. Turn left at Pleasant Valley; continue one-half mile and follow signs to winery. **Season:** Year round. **Admission:** Free. **Telephone:** (607) 569-2111.

For lodging and restaurant suggestions, contact the Schuyler County Chamber of Commerce at 1000 North Franklin Street, P.O. Box 330, Watkins Glen, N.Y. 14891. **Telephone:** (607) 535-4300.

Corning

Mankind has depended on glass for over 3,500 years, using it to form everything from drinking vessels to television tubes.

A town of about 13,000 residents located at the southwestern edge of the Finger Lakes district, Corning comes as something of a surprise. The surrounding countryside is distinctly rural, but Corning itself has a cosmopolitan air. It's really a small town with some big-city sophistication. From its restored Main Street to its world-famous glass center, Corning is a haven for shoppers and sightseers. Seldom will you visit a town where so much thought has gone into simplifying the logistics of getting from one appealing attraction to another and generally making life pleasant for the visitor.

Corning, of course, is synonymous with Corning Ware, that sturdy blue-and-white cookware that legions of Americans have given or gotten as wedding and housewarming gifts. But Corning Ware is barely even the tip of the iceberg. The real story here centers on the development of a broad variety of glass products, ranging from the utilitarian to the artistic. Mankind has depended upon glass for over 3,500 years, using it to form everything from drinking vessels to vases, optical equipment to television tubes. And, for over a century, Corning has played a vital part in the development of glass technology and design.

The Brooklyn Flint Glassworks was attracted to the Corning area in the mid-1800s, largely because plentiful supplies of anthracite coal from nearby Pennsylvania meant lower production costs. The company incorporated in 1875 as the Corning Glass Works. One of its earliest major projects was the production of bulbs for the electric lights invented by Thomas Alva Edison. Built in 1951, the **Corning Glass Center** now welcomes nearly three-quarters of a million visitors each year. The history and properties of glass are illustrated here in a huge complex devoted to the past, present, and future of glass.

The glass center maintains a large parking lot near the edge of town. During the summer months, double-decker buses transport visitors to the center for free. The buses also make stops in the restored Market Street shopping area. A helpful guide mans each bus and provides historical information about Corning along with tips on what to do during your visit. The buses make continuous loops, and you are

At the Corning Museum of Glass, you can touch the bottom of a 2000-year-old bottle found in a Roman tomb.

free to get on and off as often as you please. Parking is also available directly adjacent to the glass center, and you may find it more convenient to leave your car here during the off-season months.

You will probably want to begin with a visit to the **Corning Glass Center** itself, which has three major areas to explore. Seven galleries lead off the circular corridor that forms the spine of The Corning Museum of Glass. The exhibits in the corridor are organized chronologically. Here you will find that the first glass, known as obsidian, was formed over 40 million years ago by volcanic eruptions. Stone Age man chipped many tools and weapons from this material. The objects in the museum are young by comparison, dating back 3,500 years and culminating in contemporary pieces. You will see a footed glass vase, cut and cast in Syria or Assyria between 700 and 600 B.C. Eggshell-colored, tapered, and urn-shaped, this piece was probably traded by the Phoenicians who sailed from Sidon and Tyre (now part of Lebanon). Everywhere you look you'll see case after case of fine glass. Vessels swirled in purples and blues from Mesopotamia, Phoenician head beads (used to ward off evil and infertility), an enameled Islamic vase from the 2nd century A.D., elaborate Biedermeier glass from 18th-century Eu-

Eggshell-colored, tapered, and urn-shaped, this vase was probably traded by Phoenicians who sailed from Sidon and Tyre.

A glass harmonica plays an excerpt from Mozart's Adagio in C Major.

rope, and so on. The collection is overwhelming, both in size and depth.

There are many special exhibits too, including one devoted to forgeries and reproductions. And there are unusual pieces, like a glass harmonica that plays an excerpt from Mozart's Adagio in C major for solo glass harmonica. Overhead color videos show close-ups of glassblowers at work and of mass-production techniques (the American contribution to the history of glassmaking). You can even touch the bottom of a pale green glass bottle found in a 2,000-year-old Roman tomb. But this is only the beginning. . . .

In the Hall of Science and Industry, you'll find loads of pushbutton exhibits designed to illustrate how glass is made and how it is used in science, industry, and the home. Crank a handle to activate a treated glass pipe as a hammer and you'll discover that glass can be much tougher than it looks. Kids will enjoy scaling the fiberglass climbing unit, which has lots of compartments to hide in. Other exhibits use models and photos to show the steps Corning takes to solve a customer problem or develop a product to meet a highly specialized need. There are also live demonstrations. Watch the lampworker transform glass rods into tiny animals. Or take a seat in the comfortable auditorium, where you can watch a 30-minute live demonstration on how to make the most of glassware in cooking.

The third component of the glass center is the Steuben Glass Factory, where you will stand just a few feet away from the master craftsmen who form, polish, and engrave famous Steuben crystal. It is hot and loud here, the air filled with the hiss and clang of machinery. Overlooking the work area, there are benches on which you can sit and watch the gaffer form crystal objects from hot globs of glass. As you walk down the narrow passage edging the factory floor, you'll pass by the work stations where additional processes take place.

The glass center also has a snack bar, a café, and a series of four shops, where you can purchase everything from Corning sunglasses and postcards to unique items made by more than 50 contemporary American glass artists. Steuben pieces are found in the Designer Shop, and bargains on discontinued Corning products are always plentiful in the Consumer Shop. Allow at least three hours for your tour of the whole complex.

You may even want to return in the evening for a performance of the **Corning Summer Theatre.**

The tiny glass head of Amenhotep II dates from the 15th century B.C. and is the earliest known piece of glass sculpture in the world.

This professional theater company performs during July and August, every evening except Sunday, in the Corning Glass Auditorium at the glass center. There are Thursday and Saturday matinées as well. The fare consists of a lively assortment of popular plays and musicals, featuring familiar names from stage and screen. Check the schedule when you arrive in town. You can pick up your tickets when you visit the glass center.

Now head for Market Street, the main artery in downtown Corning. Thoroughly spruced up after a decade-long restoration effort, the street is characterized by Victorian-style brick and terra cotta architecture. The shops, restaurants, and exhibits you'll visit are housed in turn-of-the-century factories, businesses, and even a former hotel. **The Rockwell Museum,** which houses the largest collection of western art east of the Mississippi, makes its home in the former city hall. This is a good place to begin your downtown exploration.

Here you will find American paintings and bronzes by famous artists like Frederic Remington, C.M. Russell, Albert Bierstadt, and W.R. Leigh. Indian artifacts, including pottery and weavings, are also displayed. The museum has a collection of 2,000 pieces of Carder Steuben glass, which was produced in Corning from 1903 to 1933. Take a seat on one of the commodious oatmeal-colored couches while you watch videotapes describing the processes of glass formation and decoration. There is also an extensive collection of antique toys, including a splendid Blue Comet train set manufactured by Lionel in the 1930s, complete with bathrooms. Save some time for the museum shop, too, where you can try on fine leather cowboy boots. The shop also stocks hand-woven blankets and rag rugs, clay baskets, silver and turquoise jewelry, and reproduction kachina dolls, along with prints, books, and postcards.

Speaking of shops, take a peek inside **Kriss Kringle's Christmas Shop** on Market Street. This cheerful store is simply stuffed with Christmas ornaments and decorations. Baskets overflowing with ornaments cluster at the feet of full-size trees decorated in whimsical themes. Many of the delicate pieces are displayed on lovely oak cabinets and cases. Whether your tastes lean toward the traditional terra cotta angel or the more contemporary Santa Claus on a unicycle, you're sure to find something special for your tree. Ornaments are made of glass, wood, bread dough, straw, papier-mâché,

David and Meredith Baxter Birney in Talley's Folly *at the Corning Summer Theatre.*

CORNING SUMMER THEATRE

Baskets overflowing with Christmas ornaments cluster at the feet of full-size trees decorated in whimsical themes.

pewter, gold, and lots of other materials, and many are imported from Italy and Germany.

If you want to find a perfect piece of glass to take home as a remembrance of your visit to Corning, stop in at **The Glass Menagerie,** on East Market Street. You'll recognize the storefront by the 20-foot-long, leaded stained glass window in the façade, which was handmade in the Corning area. There are exquisite glass paperweights from around the world, many of them signed and dated. There are hundreds of glass bells to choose from, and hundreds of glass animals from near and far, including pieces by local artists. Whether you are looking for a lead crystal pendant or a piece of free-form studio glass, you are bound to find an irresistible treasure.

If you would like to see studio glass made, drop by the **Vitrix Hot Glass Studio** on West Market Street. Watch skilled craftsmen blow glass, using ancient techniques to create distinctive contemporary designs. In the gallery, you can purchase work by glass artist Tom Buechner, co-owner and principal designer at Vitrix. Pieces vary from hand-blown Christmas ornaments to free-form paperweights and elegant perfume bottles.

Now head for **The Wine Center,** located in the old Baron Steuben Hotel. Here you'll see a series of educational exhibits focusing on the history and production of wine. You'll learn how the develop-

Glass artist Thomas Buechner of Vitrix Hot Glass Studio works on his latest design.

ment of the cork stopper in the 18th century revolutionized winemaking. And you'll discover that winemaking has a considerable history even in America. Early colonists and 19th-century immigrants grew wine grapes coast to coast until Prohibition put a lid on their activity. During that notorious era, some wineries survived by manufacturing sacramental wines. Others turned to wine-filled chocolates to weather the storm.

Actually a small museum, The Wine Center contains some intriguing wine-related artifacts, like the 18th-century Dutch tavern bottle decorated in polychrome after a painting by Rembrandt. A fellow in a plumed hat raises his goblet with one hand and gives the barmaid a friendly pat on the rump with the other. Here you will also learn how to properly open and serve a bottle of what Louis Pasteur called "the most hygienic and faithful of beverages." In the tasting room, with its inlaid tile floor and long walnut and mahogany bar, you can sample wines from 14 different New York State wineries and purchase your favorites.

Try to plan your visit to The Wine Center to coincide with a fit of hunger. **Ice Cream Works** is located on the bottom floor in the same building and shouldn't be missed. With its Tiffany-style lighting, lace curtains, abundance of mirrors, and long marble counter, it just reeks of Victorian ambiance. Take a seat at the counter or choose one of the round marble-topped tables, some covered with pink tablecloths. The ice cream parlor is open for breakfast and lunch and has a well-stocked delicatessen counter. After satisfying your nutritional needs, you'll want to try something really sinful — maybe "The Turtle," hot butterscotch with five scoops of butter pecan ice cream topped with hot fudge, whipped cream, and a cherry. All of the sundaes can be ordered with frozen yogurt instead of ice cream, if you like. What a way to wrap up a day in Corning!

During Prohibition some wineries survived by manufacturing sacramental wines, while others turned to wine-filled chocolates.

ACCESS

CORNING. To reach Corning, follow I-88 west to Binghamton; pick up Route 17 and continue west to Corning.

CORNING GLASS CENTER. Directions: The main parking area is located on Centerway; you will see signs from Route 17. Free tour buses transport visitors from the parking area to the glass center and the historic Market Street area during the summer months. **Season:** Year round. **Admission:** Charged. **Telephone:** (607) 974-8271.

CORNING SUMMER THEATRE. Directions: Located at the Corning Glass Center. **Season:** July and August, Monday through Saturday. **Admission:** Charged. **Telephone:** (607) 936-4634.

THE ROCKWELL MUSEUM. Directions: The museum is housed in the Old City Hall in downtown Corning. Take Route 17 to Route 414 (Cedar Street). Museum is located at the intersection of the two routes. There is a municipal parking lot adjacent to the museum, which is also accessible by the free tour buses. **Season:** Year round. **Admission:** Charged. **Telephone:** (607) 937-5386.

KRISS KRINGLE'S CHRISTMAS SHOP. Directions: Located at 73-75 East Market Street in Corning. **Season:** Year round. **Admission:** Free. **Telephone:** (607) 936-8000.

THE GLASS MENAGERIE. Directions: Located at 37 East Market Street. **Season:** Year round. **Admission:** Free. **Telephone:** (607) 962-6700.

VITRIX HOT GLASS STUDIO. Directions: Located in the Hawkes Building at 77 West Market Street. **Season:** Year round. **Admission:** Free. **Telephone:** (607) 936-8707.

THE WINE CENTER. Directions: Located in Baron Steuben Place, at the corner of Centerway and Market Street in downtown Corning. **Season:** Year round. **Admission:** Free. **Telephone:** (607) 962-6072.

ICE CREAM WORKS. Directions: Located in Baron Steuben Place, at the corner of Centerway and Market Street in downtown Corning. **Season:** Year round. **Admission:** Free. **Telephone:** (607) 962-8481.

For lodging and restaurant suggestions in the area, contact the Chamber of Commerce, 42 East Market Street, Corning, N.Y. 14830. **Telephone:** (607) 936-4686.

Rochester

If you love museums, you shouldn't miss Rochester. While the city itself is not particularly attractive, you'll soon discover that its buildings house some truly outstanding treasures.

With a population of nearly a quarter of a million, Rochester is the third largest city in the state. Perhaps best known as the home of Eastman Kodak, the city also serves as the headquarters for other major corporations, such as Bausch and Lomb and Xerox. We think the best way to really get a taste of Rochester is to combine an insider's look at contemporary American industry with a strong dose of culture.

George Eastman founded what is now called the Eastman Kodak Company in 1880, right here in Rochester. By this time he had already invented a machine for coating the glass plates used in cameras. In 1884 he introduced flexible roll film and in 1888 he started producing a camera so inexpensive that it brought photography into the hands of millions of moderate-income Americans. Eastman died in 1932, but the company that he began continued to grow. Today, Kodak is the world's largest manufacturer of photographic products.

The company offers two plant tours, which introduce visitors to the people, products, and plants that make up the industry. The Kodak Park Division is the company's largest plant, often referred to as "a city within a city." The park is over seven miles in length and sprawls over 2,000 acres of land in downtown Rochester and adjacent Greece, employing more than 28,000 people in approximately 200 manufacturing buildings. Nearly a thousand kinds of film are produced here, more than 270 kinds of photographic paper, and over 900 chemical formulas used in processing film and paper. You begin to get the idea. The numbers are very BIG here. Kodak Park is also the home of the company's largest United States color print and processing laboratories.

The **Kodak Factory Tour,** which lasts a little more than an hour, begins in the visitor lobby, where you'll see a short film introducing you to the company. Then you'll board a bus and make your way through the huge compound, which contains its own fire department (three fire stations and over a hundred full-time firemen), three electrical plants,

In 1888 George Eastman produced a camera so inexpensive that it brought photography into the hands of millions of Americans.

and medical facilities staffed around the clock by 70 doctors and nurses. The "city" has a food service department that operates 31 cafeterias, preparing 23,000 meals a day. (As a tour guest, you're entitled to buy lunch in the Kodak Park Service Dining Room, adjacent to the visitor lobby.) The plant also has its own railroad with 19 miles of track, 43 rail cars, and four diesel locomotives. Your tour guide will point out the buildings where various products are manufactured, as you drive through an industrial panorama of pipes, machinery, buildings, and trucks. The park even produces its own weekly newspaper.

The automatic foot washer washes the soles of your shoes before you enter a lint-free environment.

Now get off the bus and walk through the automatic foot washer (you get to keep your shoes on; it just washes dirt off the bottoms because you're entering an environment that has to be kept as lint-free as possible) and into the film-processing building. You'll see another slide presentation here. This one takes you into a darkroom and explains the steps involved in processing film. Huge rolls of film are cut into strips, sprocketed, then cut again into lengths of 24 and 36 exposures in spooling machines — and all this work takes place in the dark. You'll pass quickly through a simulated darkroom, where you discover that workers really do have to do their jobs by feel, which means they experience virtually no eyestrain. Then take a walk through the factory, where you'll see hundreds of those familiar little yellow film boxes making their way through a system of machines and conveyor belts during the packaging process.

By the time the tour ends — and you'll get an Instamatic snapshot of yourself to take home as a memento — you'll know more than you ever dreamed about Kodak. For example, did you know that Kodak is the largest producer of floppy disks in the United States, as well as the largest producer of Vitamin E? Well, that's just the beginning. . . .

For a different perspective on George Eastman, head straight for the **International Museum of Photography at George Eastman House.** Eastman built the 50-room, Georgian-style mansion in 1905, and it remains the largest private house ever constructed in Rochester. The museum has the largest collection of 19th-century photography in the world and just about all the major photographers of the past 150 years are represented here. You'll see how photographs were used to capture nature, make portraits, and record history. You'll also see some of the first stop-action sequences ever done,

Take a close look at Kodak's manufacturing and print-processing operation on the Kodak Factory Tour.

these being the predecessors of motion pictures. In the 20th-century galleries, you'll see works by famous photographers like Alfred Stieglitz, Edward Steichen, and Ansel Adams. Also on display are collections of cameras, lenses, and motion picture equipment, along with exhibits that explain different photographic processes.

The museum contains a "discovery room," where visitors can participate in hands-on activities designed to clarify the concepts involved in photography and filmmaking. Using the camera obscura, visitors compose and draw their own images. You might make your own pinhole camera or use light-sensitive paper to create photograms or sunprints.

Just a couple of blocks away, at the **Rochester Museum and Science Center,** you can view exhibits devoted to natural history, anthropology, human biology, and regional history. Wander down "Main Street" and peer into period rooms depicting domestic and commercial life in 19th-century Rochester. The young ladies' seminary is set up for art class,

Make your own pinhole camera or use light-sensitive paper to create photograms or sunprints.

and at the Asa Prid Tin Shop you'll get a glimpse of the "latest" in metal bathtubs and butter churns.

You'll see a rich collection of Indian artifacts, along with a slide show focusing on the customs of the New York Iroquois, illustrated with paintings by a Seneca artist. As you examine a real Seneca log cabin, it may come as a surprise to discover that the Indians copied this design from typical early dwellings of white settlers. An exhibit centering on the development of bark canoes and skin boats is accompanied by 17th-century quotes regarding canoe etiquette: "Do not begin to paddle unless you are inclined to continue paddling. . . . Be careful not to annoy anyone in the canoe with your hat."

"Be careful not to annoy anyone in the canoe with your hat."

Other exhibits include the anatomical woman, in which the TAM (transparent anatomical mannequin) gives us a look inside her illuminated plastic body as she explains that "muscles are like rubber bands. They pull on bones to make them move." There is also a small but intriguing exhibit with pointers on how to develop an insect collection and prepare specimens. You can use a magnifying glass to examine beetles, moths, and butterflies close up.

The museum's Strasenburgh Planetarium offers daily star shows under a 60-foot dome. Seasonal mini shows key visitors in on what they can expect to see in the night skies of western New York at that particular time of the year. These presentations are often teamed up with feature shows centering on a particular topic, such as "The Space Shuttle, An American Adventure" and "Galaxy," which takes viewers to the center of the Milky Way. Children under five are not admitted to most of the regular planetarium shows, but neither are they neglected. There is a generous schedule of special shows designed with the preschooler in mind. Telephone ahead for specifics.

The Memorial Art Gallery of the University of Rochester houses an outstanding collection of artifacts from ancient Egyptian, Greek, Roman, and pre-Columbian civilizations, all in a palatial Italian Renaissance-style building. There are some fine examples of medieval art; 19th-century American paintings and folk art and contemporary American prints; 19th- and 20th-century French paintings; and an outdoor sculpture garden that visitors can explore as well.

We are thoroughly enamored of Rochester's newest museum, the **Margaret Woodbury Strong Museum,** which interprets social and cultural forces, great and small, that contributed to the changing face of America in the 19th and early 20th centuries, a period when our country evolved from a rural, agrarian society into an urban, industrial one, served by complex transportation and communication systems and characterized by the growth of mass-production techniques.

The artifacts are displayed according to subject and cover everything from the ethnic and racial prejudice shown against Chinese immigrants, as reflected in 19th-century toys and political cartoons, to the premiums that Victorian families could acquire by saving product labels — the enterprising child could furnish an entire dollhouse with folding paper furniture acquired at no cost by saving labels from Dunham's Coconut. In a display devoted to advertising and the mass market, we see a poster showing a broken-down horsedrawn wagon juxtaposed against one in good shape. The driver of the former says to the driver of the latter: "If I had used Frazer Axle Grease, I would not have this trouble . . . ," to which his compassionate friend replies: "My friend, don't cry! Get your wagon fixed up and then use Frazer Axle Grease Petroleum Grease — both black and white will run your axles every time."

Whether the exhibit focuses on patent furniture, like folding chairs with carpeted upholstery (more than 150 patents were issued for such items from 1855 through 1870) or on health problems like "neurasthenia" (nervous breakdown, thought to be caused by overuse of the brain and excessive expenditure of nervous energy), the items are displayed in uncluttered alcoves with meticulous labeling. Displays center on fashion, funeral habits, child care, and just about every other aspect of 19th-century commercial and domestic life. Many exhibits are accompanied by items that visitors can touch. These are also labeled in braille, and include everything from 19th-century kitchen tools to a wood-and-leather ice skate, a mold for making doll hands to an Art Nouveau furniture fragment.

Located in an expansive contemporary building, the museum is well known for its doll collection, which numbers nearly 20,000 pieces and also includes hundreds of antique dollhouses, toys, and miniatures. Upstairs you will find case after case containing collections of Flow Blue china, American art pottery, cut and pressed glass, Victorian ladies' handcrafts, and much more. The collections were amassed by Margaret Woodbury Strong, a wealthy Rochester woman with a passion for collecting.

Just about every aspect of 19th-century life, from fashion to furniture to funeral habits, is presented at the Margaret Woodbury Strong Museum.

The enterprising Victorian child could furnish an entire dollhouse by saving labels from Dunham's Coconut.

More than 50 categories of objects are represented in all.

If you are visiting Rochester with children, you may want to contact the museum in advance to get a schedule of special workshops designed to bring the Victorian period alive for young people. While your young ones learn to play parlor games like the Graces and Jack Straws, you can wander through the collections on your own. On leaving the museum, you might want to take time out for a hot dog in **Manhattan Square Park,** directly across from the main entrance to the museum. There is a playground here with oversized slides and wooden climbing equipment. Older children will enjoy climbing the towering metal space-frame observation tower. There's even a wading pool with waterfalls where kids can cool off.

The **Seneca Park Zoo** is another good stop for families. There are about 500 animals here, representing nearly 200 species. Some come from as nearby as the Adirondacks, while others hail from as far away as Africa. Animals included in this mostly cold-climate collection include polar bears, a yak, a Siberian tiger, reindeer, and assorted small mammals. The zoo has lots of greenery, making it a pleasant place to wander. In the free-flight room, colorful birds fly about in a tropical setting, with no bars to separate them from you. There are farm animals to pet in the mini zoo, and a more extensive children's zoo is currently in the planning stages. With a snack bar, two picnic areas, and lots of greenery, the zoo is a pleasant place to take a break from more formal sightseeing.

In the free-flight room, colorful birds fly about in a tropical setting, with no bars to separate them from you.

ACCESS

ROCHESTER. Follow I-90 (New York State Thruway) to I-490, which forms the Inner Loop, circling the downtown area.

KODAK FACTORY TOUR. Directions: From I-490, follow I-390 north to Route 104 (Ridge Road). Travel east on Route 104 to Kodak Park. **Season:** Year round. **Admission:** Free. **Telephone:** (716) 722-2465. **Note:** Tours commence twice a day, at 9:30 A.M. and 1:30 P.M. Tours are also available at the same times at Kodak's Elmgrove Plant located off I-490.

INTERNATIONAL MUSEUM OF PHOTOGRAPHY AT GEORGE EASTMAN HOUSE. Directions: Located at 900 East Avenue. **Season:** Year round. **Admission:** Charged. **Telephone:** (716) 271-3361. **Note:** Discovery room is open limited hours. Call for specifics.

Polar bear cubs get some southern exposure at the Seneca Park Zoo.

ROCHESTER MUSEUM AND SCIENCE CENTER. Directions: Located at 657 East Avenue. **Season:** Year round. **Admission:** Charged. **Telephone:** (716) 271-1880.

MEMORIAL ART GALLERY OF THE UNIVERSITY OF ROCHESTER. Directions: Located at 490 University Avenue. **Season:** Year round. **Admission:** Charged. **Telephone:** (716) 275-3081.

MARGARET WOODBURY STRONG MUSEUM. Directions: Located at One Manhattan Square. **Season:** Year round. **Admission:** Charged. **Telephone:** (716) 263-2700.

MANHATTAN SQUARE PARK. Directions: Located across from the main entrance to the Margaret Woodbury Strong Museum. **Season:** Year round. **Admission:** Free. **Telephone:** None.

SENECA PARK ZOO. Directions: Travel east on Route 104 to St. Paul Street. Turn left on St. Paul and continue to park entrance, on your left. **Season:** Year round. **Admission:** Small admission fee charged. **Telephone:** (716) 342-2744.

For lodging and restaurant suggestions, write to the Rochester–Monroe County Visitor Information Center at 120 East Main Street, Rochester, N.Y. 14604. **Telephone:** (716) 546-3070.

Mumford and More

T ake your time exploring country roads, making your way past acres of cornfields and through small towns as you travel the northern part of the Finger Lakes region. The places you'll visit are all located an hour's drive or less from the urban intensity of bustling Rochester, yet they will seem thousands of miles removed.

The big attraction on this trip is the **Genesee Country Village and Museum,** a living-history museum that re-creates the characteristic tempo and way of life of 19th-century upstate New York. You'll probably want to spend the better part of the day here — wandering in and out of the 50 buildings that make up the village, communing with the resident farm animals, enjoying the period gardens, and watching craftsmen at work.

Genesee Country is the part of the state that stretches from the Finger Lakes up to the Niagara Frontier. "Genesee" is the Iroquois word for "pleasant valley," and was bestowed by the Indians who once made their homes here. The village chronicles the accomplishments of the 19th-century Americans who settled here, progressing from rudimentary log homes to luxurious mansions in just 25 years.

You'll begin your visit at the Flint Hill Country Store at the base of Great Meadow. You can stroll across the meadow, perhaps stopping in at the **Gallery of Sporting Art,** where over 500 original paintings, prints, and bronze sculptures interpret man's relationship with birds and animals. Then be sure to amble past the magnificent Victorian bandstand. The meadow is also the setting for a series of outdoor bronze sculptures, each the work of a different contemporary American artist. If the weather is hot or your feet reluctant, climb aboard the tractor-drawn trolley that circles the village, picking up and dropping off visitors at convenient points.

The main buildings in the village are attended by costumed interpreters, who introduce visitors to the families who once lived here as well as to the architectural and decorative features of each building. In the Octagon House (1853), imported from Friendship, New York, we learn that, as well as being decorative the cupola provided light and ventilation. (From the outside the house looks just like a green wedding cake, with its gingerbread trim

"Genesee" is the Iroquois word for "pleasant valley."

The Altay Store, one of 50 buildings you can investigate as you go from farm to market at Genesee Country Village.

"frosting" and three "layers.") Notice that the marble-patterned wallpaper in the main hall was applied in blocks rather than in strips; that's to maximize the effect, giving a real feeling that the walls were indeed constructed from marble slabs. The dining room in the nearby Hamilton House, a post-Civil War Italianate villa, is decorated with no less than eight different patterns of wallpaper. If you've visited George Eastman's opulent mansion in Rochester (see page 138), you'll appreciate what a long way he came when you visit his birthplace, which has been moved to the village. A simple mid-19th-century home, it has grass mats on the floor and a crumb cloth under the dining room table. The window shades are painted with scenes of sailboats and lakes (facing outdoors), and there is a large soapstone sink in the kitchen.

The pioneer farmstead, an 1809-vintage log cabin, represents basic rural simplicity, while the post-and-beam Jones Farmhouse, built just a decade later, testifies to the improved lot of the Genesee farmer, who enjoyed luxuries like stenciled walls and a spacious kitchen (with bunches of yellow tansy hung in the doorways to discourage flies and fleas).

The village offers insight into 19th-century commercial as well as domestic life. When you visit the office of attorney George Hastings, its walls lined with his leatherbound law books, you'll find that the gentleman handled everything from criminal cases to debt collection. He also drafted wills and deeds and provided counsel in marriage disputes. You'll also learn that if you had lived in Victorian times, you would have gone to the drugstore to purchase art supplies and window glass as well as remedies for your ailments. The early 19th-century pharmacist and the village doctor often competed with one another, both prescribing and selling medicines. Over in the printshop, the village printer assembles a broadside as he explains how he uses composing sticks to form lines of print.

In Victorian times, you would have gone to the drugstore to purchase art supplies and window glass.

For gardening enthusiasts, the village also offers the Livingstone-Backus House formal garden (planted with tree shrubs and flowers that were sold at the Monroe Garden and Nursery in the 1830s) and the curvilinear gardens flanking the Octagon House, typical of the "picturesque" gardens favored in the mid-19th century. There is also a lovely herb garden, where the village cooks harvest many of the seasonings they use in the soups and stews prepared daily. The cooks also use the bounty supplied by the orchards and heirloom vegetable gardens found here and there in the village. The resident craftsmen make use of the flowers grown in the dye garden adjacent to the Amherst-Humphrey House to color their yarns.

You're welcome to bring your own picnic to the village. If you choose to purchase refreshments here, you will find sandwiches, soups, and desserts served at the Depot Cafeteria, along with beer and ale during the summer months and on spring and fall weekends. Or you can take a restful break at the lovely Victorian Refreshment Pavilion. The gray structure, decorated with airy pink lattice work, surrounds a pretty garden, where brick pathways wind around flowerbeds and a central fountain. Tables are situated around the courtyard, and waitresses in lacy white aprons serve hot and cold lunches as operetta music plays in the background. Treat yourself to a leisurely lunch of seafood salad and fresh strawberry shortcake, or stop in for just a lemonade or a glass of wine.

Waitresses in lacy white aprons serve lunch in the pavilion, as operetta music plays in the background.

We've only begun to describe what the village has to offer. We haven't even touched upon the carriage barn, with its collection of horsedrawn vehicles that traveled early roads. When you pass through the tollhouse leading from the Great Meadow to the village square, you'll learn that by 1875 nearly 3,000 miles of plank roads were in use in

Ranks of 60-year-old red pines tower over the Beaver Trail at Cumming Nature Center.

New York State. Private companies constructed and owned them, and people had to pay to use them. The sign outside this particular tollhouse notes a charge of three to four cents per mile for a vehicle and animal, but only one to two cents per mile for "a score of sheep, swine, or neat cattle."

The village sponsors a wonderful assortment of special events from mid-May through mid-October, everything from a highland gathering with four bagpipe bands to a re-creation of the Battle of Gettysburg. Enjoy an agricultural fair or a firemen's muster, or watch the antics of a one-ring circus similar to the small family circuses popular in the 19th century. Some of these events require advance tickets. Write to Genesee Country Museum, Mumford, N.Y. 14511 for schedule and details.

The **Cumming Nature Center** in Naples is a different kind of outdoor museum. Here you can explore six miles of walking trails that pass through woodlands and wetlands. Begin at the visitor center, where you take a look at slide shows and exhibits designed to introduce you to natural cycles and ecosystems. Then explore the thematic trails, perhaps

Private companies constructed and owned the plank roads, which people had to pay to use.

climbing an observation tower to overlook a beaver pond, or making the acquaintance of a yoke of oxen at the reconstructed 18th-century homestead. Learn about theories of forest management as you walk the conservation trail, which leads to a working sawmill. In the winter you can travel the trails on skis or snowshoes (both can be rented here), and during sugaring season you can enjoy pancakes served with maple syrup made right at the center.

If you like camping or simply want to hike in the woods, pay a visit to **Letchworth State Park,** about half an hour's drive from Mumford. The park features the Genesee Gorge, miles of deep canyon with the Genesee River winding below, formed when glaciers blocked an early riverbed. The 14,350-acre park is one of the most notable examples of waterfall and gorge scenery in the eastern United States. The highest of the three waterfalls rises over 100 feet, and cliffs bordering the river sometimes reach heights of nearly 600 feet.

The most popular winter activity is "tubing," sliding down the hills on inner tubes.

Park facilities include rental cabins, tent and trailer sites, hiking trails, fishing areas, and two swimming pools. Guided whitewater rafting trips through the park, covering six miles in two hours, are also available. If you are experienced in whitewater canoeing, you can secure a special permit at park administration headquarters that will allow you to travel the Genesee River independently (two or more canoes must travel together). Winter activities include winter camping, ice skating, and cross-country skiing. The most popular winter activity is "tubing," sliding down the hills on inner tubes. Indeed, tubes are the only kind of sliding equipment permitted here. Snowmobiling is also allowed, in specified areas.

There is also a small Museum of Pioneer and Indian History, with exhibits focusing on early regional settlement. A restored Seneca Indian Council House sits near the grave of Mary Jemison, a white woman who was adopted by two Seneca women after Indians killed most of her family. She eventually married a Seneca chief and assumed the role of a Seneca woman, settling here in the Genesee Valley. Some of Mary's possessions, such as her teapot, are exhibited in the museum.

The park also sponsors weekly evening concerts in the summer months, including big band music, jazz bands, and an appearance by the Buffalo Philharmonic Orchestra. Evening lectures at the Trailside Lodge introduce visitors to local geology and history.

For a very different type of entertainment, head for the **Finger Lakes Race Track** in Canandaigua. Admission to see the thoroughbreds run is less than the price of a movie. Of course, when it comes to betting ... Post time is 1:00 P.M., and you can catch the action from the grandstand or from the terrace dining room. Television monitors show simulcasts of classic races like the Kentucky Derby and the Preakness and Belmont Stakes, adding to the fun. You can bet on these and other major stakes races from New York Racing Association tracks right here. Good luck!

ACCESS

GENESEE COUNTRY VILLAGE AND MUSEUM. Directions: From I-90 (New York State Thruway), take Exit 46. Follow I-390 south to Route 253; then take Route 253 west to Route 383. Take Route 383 into Mumford, following signs to museum. **Season:** Mid-May through late October. **Admission:** Charged. **Telephone:** (716) 538-2887.

CUMMING NATURE CENTER. Directions: From I-90 (New York State Thruway), take Exit 46. Follow I-390 south to Route 20. Turn left onto Route 20, then right on Route 37 and continue to Honeoye. Turn right on East Lake Road, left on Pinewood Hill Road, then right on Gulick Road. Continue seven miles to center. **Season:** Year round. **Admission:** Charged. **Telephone:** (716) 374-6160.

LETCHWORTH STATE PARK. Directions: From I-90 (New York State Thruway), take Exit 46. Follow I-390 south to Exit 10. Take Route 20 west into Avon. Follow Route 39 south to Route 36. Continue south on Route 36 to Mt. Morris entrance. **Season:** Year round. **Admission:** Charged. **Telephone:** (716) 493-2611.

FINGER LAKES RACE TRACK. Directions: From I-90 (New York State Thruway), take Exit 44. Continue one mile south on Route 332 to the track. **Season:** End of March through early November. **Admission:** Charged. **Telephone:** (716) 924-3232.

For lodging and restaurant suggestions, contact the Convention and Visitors Bureau at 55 Saint Paul Street, Rochester, N.Y. 14604.

Allegany State Park

T he hills that run through **Allegany State Park** are high and steep, the valleys deep and narrow. Originally established by legislative act in 1921, the park began with 7,000 acres. Today it encompasses well over 60,000 acres in the southwestern part of the state. The Erie and Seneca Indian nations once occupied this land. Since that time lumber and chemical companies have exploited its resources, farmers have attempted to cultivate it, and the Society of Friends (Quakers) has worked to introduce the practice of temperance here.

Today the park operates under a policy that balances recreational development with the control and protection of wildlife and other natural resources. It contains two large lakes, a maze of streams ("allegany" is an Indian word meaning "beautiful waters"), and nearly 70 miles of hiking trails. It is a place for swimming and fishing, bird-watching and hunting. It is also a place for enjoying the wilderness with relative ease, where you don't have to be an avid outdoorsman or proficient camper to have a good experience. And, no matter what the season, there is always activity going on here.

This part of the state experiences long, cold winters. Light snow usually begins to fall in mid-September and the heavier stuff arrives around Thanksgiving, continuing through April and tapering off in May. Local tradition holds that snow can appear here at any month of the year, and skeptics were put in their place on July 1, 1979, when a dusting of flakes added credibility to the story. The park maintains some winterized cabins and 12 miles of snowmobiling trails. Ice skating is available, too. The park also includes the **Art Roscoe Ski Touring Area,** which contains five cross-country ski trails, varying in difficulty and length. The ski area includes a warming hut and rental equipment is available.

The park offers the perfect family outing, be it for a day, a week, or even longer. There are two major recreational areas, Red House and Quaker. Red House is dominated by a huge English Tudor-style building, overlooking the lake that was built by Civilian Conservation Corps and WPA workers in 1928. This building is the center of park activity, containing rental offices, a small natural history museum, a restaurant, and a gift shop. This is the place to ask questions and seek advice, whether you

Skeptics were put in their place on July 1, 1979, when a dusting of snow confirmed local opinion that it can snow in the park at any time of year.

want to know about special park naturalist programs or need help in choosing an appropriate hiking trail. If you want to try your luck at catching delicious brook trout, make sure you have a valid New York State fishing license along and pick up a special permit from the Allegany Park Commission (at the Park Police Office in the Red House Administration Building) before casting your line (the season runs from April 1 through September 30 each year). This is also the place to inquire about hunting regulations, if you're lured by the prospect of wild turkey and whitetail deer.

Red House maintains 144 cabins, over half of which are winterized, allowing year-round use. The cabins we saw were small green cottages, each with a front porch. They're primitive, with no indoor plumbing, and are located in tight clusters. Tent and trailer sites are also available.

Red House Lake offers a pretty swimming beach, where the lawn comes down almost to the edge of the water. A miniature golf course adjacent to the beach is popular with people of just about any age. At **The Boathouse,** adjacent to the beach, you can rent rowboats, fishing poles, and bicycles, along with badminton, tennis, softball, and volleyball equipment. Rentals are available on a daily or hourly basis, and you'll need to leave a major credit card and your driver's license or car registration as a security deposit. You can buy live bait here, too, stuff like mealworms and softshell crayfish.

Experience nature with the comforts of home close at hand at Allegany State Park.

Treat yourself to one of the "wildlife coffees," like a "Hummingbird" (laced with Grand Marnier) or a "Bear" (with a hit of Jack Daniels).

The Quaker Area, located in the original section of the park, offers cabins and a few campsites, but not for winter use. (The newest camping area in the park is Cain Hollow–Quaker Lake, which has 164 tent and trailer sites and is within walking distance of the lake.) Quaker Lake, which has a swimming area and a snack bar, is the only open body of water in the park where fishing is allowed year round, making it popular with ice fishermen. There is also an outdoor amphitheater located here, where movies are shown and cultural events held during the summer.

If you plan to stay overnight in the park, advance planning is a must. During the peak period (the end of June to Labor Day), campsites and cabins must be reserved for one- or two-week periods. Per night rentals are available at other times of the year. The park begins accepting reservation applications January 1 for summer camping, and October 1 for winter accommodations. Write for a rate sheet and application.

The park sponsors an interpretive program that runs Monday through Saturday during the summer, with more than 10 activities scheduled daily. Naturalists lead visitors on a tour of a beaver colony, a fossil hunt, a bird walk, a star watch, and even a 25-mile bike trip. Music, movies, and slide shows are also part of the program, and there are always several events just right for children.

If you are an economy-minded traveler, you'll be gratified to know that the daily fee for parking and park entry is waived after 5:00 P.M. This means that if you are staying elsewhere in the area, you can come for an evening swim, enjoy a picnic supper, attend an early evening naturalist program, and wrap it all up with a slide show or movie in the Quaker area amphitheater, all at no charge.

The park has two stores, one at Red House and one at Quaker Lake, both of which cater to picnickers and campers. You can pick up everything from ice to batteries, propane to souvenirs, ice cream to more serious food, without ever leaving the park. You can even eat "out" in style. **The Red House Inn,** with its parquet floors, butcher-block tables, and abundance of greenery, was originally built in the early 1800s. The fare includes Southern-fried chicken, baked stuffed trout, and prime rib. There's also a children's menu. Treat yourself to one of the "wildlife coffees," like a "Hummingbird" (coffee laced with Grand Marnier) or a "Bear" (coffee with a hit of Jack Daniels).

Allegany State Park offers a multitude of activity options all year round. There is plenty for the avid outdoorsman and the athletically minded to do, but there is also ample opportunity for low-key communing with nature for the visitor who prefers a less strenuous visit. But no matter how much there is to do in the huge park, it would be a shame to leave the area without making a stop or two in nearby Salamanca, the only city in the world, we are told, to be located entirely on an Indian reservation. It is a part of the Allegany Indian Reservation, which extends north from the Pennsylvania border upriver to Vandalia, New York, containing 30,469 acres of land.

Here you can visit the **Seneca-Iroquois National Museum,** devoted to the preservation and interpretation of the artifacts, cultural treasures, and way of life of the Iroquois people. Special emphasis is placed on the Seneca Nation of Indians (SNI), the federally recognized tribe that holds title to the reservation. Seneca social patterns were based on the clan system. The importance of clan association is expressed throughout the museum collections. The SNI includes eight clans: the Wolf, Turtle, Bear, Beaver, Deer, Heron, Snipe, and Hawk.

Museum exhibits illustrate different facets of Seneca and Iroquois life. Visitors can wander independently or take a one-hour guided tour (strongly recommended). On the tour, the guides (all of whom are of Seneca descent) explain the symbolism of the artifacts and tell stories related to Indian culture and history.

We learn about Indian ritual through objects like a Huron alliance belt, a cornplanter condolence belt, and a nomination belt.

The artifacts are attractively displayed, and vary from the finely crafted silver brooches and beadwork of the Iroquois woman's costume to an elegant contemporary soapstone carving of a bear and turtle. There are archeological materials like pipes and drills made of stone and awls and combs of bone. We learn about Indian ritual through objects like a Huron alliance belt, a cornplanter condolence belt, and a nomination belt. There is also a full-size Seneca lodge, constructed of bark and saplings. Be sure to look at the actual documents that have shaped the history of the area, including the Pickering 1794 treaty, which established the three reservations on which the Senecas live today, including this one.

At the beginning or end of your visit, you will be shown a 12-minute, triple-screen slide show, summarizing the history of the SNI and providing a look at contemporary Seneca life. SNI, you will discover, was formed in 1848 in the aftermath of a revolution that overthrew the chief system and replaced it with a constitution calling for elected officials, a form of government that continues today.

In the small, attractive museum shop, you can purchase high-quality handcrafted items made by contemporary Seneca artisans. We saw beaded jewelry, dolls, reproduction horn rattles, and handsome stationery, but what most captured our hearts was the tiny pair of hand-tanned deerhide baby moccasins trimmed with white rabbit fur.

While in Salamanca, train buffs should make a stop at the **Salamanca Rail Museum,** located in the restored Buffalo, Rochester, and Pittsburgh depot at the north end of Main Street. Contrary to popular belief, "Salamanca" is not an Indian name. Instead, it was the name of a Spanish count who invested heavily in the Erie Railroad, which played an important part in the history of the city. The station was built in 1912, and today it is an authentic restoration of a small urban passenger station. Made of brick and sandstone, with lofty arches over the doors, the interior literally gleams. Two stories high, the main waiting room has splendid red oak wainscoting and a narrow-board oak floor. The ceiling is spectacular — "The fellows lay on their backs on the scaffolding for seven weeks to get that done!" boasts a staff member — you'll just have to see it yourself to understand!

The museum was developed and is staffed entirely by volunteers, who are eager to "talk trains" with fellow railroad buffs. Here visitors can examine objects like conductor hats (considered a symbol of authority, these vintage examples sport brass plaques on the brim reading "Pullman Conductor" or "Brakeman"), ID cards, timetables, and tickets and rulebooks from the Baltimore & Ohio Railroad, the Erie Railroad, the Silver Lake Railroad Company, and others. Equipment includes bells, lanterns, wooden line telephones, and switch keys.

The exhibits are spread throughout the refurbished waiting room (with its polished wooden seats), the baggage room, and the "Ladies' Retiring Room." The ticket office comes equipped with Western Union cable and telegraph forms. Before leaving, you'll want to explore the several pieces of rolling stock on the grounds outside. The day we visited, a retired conductor busied himself sprucing up an old caboose with a fresh coat of trim paint. Now a museum volunteer, he was delighted to take time out to talk trains with us. We learned that he

The ceiling is spectacular: "The fellows lay on their backs on scaffolding for seven weeks to get that done!"

Yesterday's commuters used cars like these to catch the train at what is now the Salamanca Rail Museum.

favored the cupola caboose, with its elevated seats for the conductors and flagmen, over the bay window caboose, which offered less visibility. We headed back to our campsite feeling richer for having gained insight into an important part of Salamanca's heritage.

ACCESS:

ALLEGANY STATE PARK. To reach the main entrance to the park, follow Route 17 west to Exit 19. Follow signs to entrance.

CAMPSITE AND CABIN RENTALS. Season: Year round. **Admission:** Charged. **Telephone:** Red House — (716) 354-2545; Quaker Area — (716) 354-2182.

ART ROSCOE SKI TOURING AREA. Directions: Follow signs from Red House Area. **Season:** November through April, depending on snow conditions. **Admission:** Park admission. **Telephone:** (716) 354-2545.

THE BOATHOUSE. Directions: Located in Red House Recreational Area. **Season:** April through Labor Day. **Admission:** Fees charged. **Telephone:** (716) 354-4041.

THE RED HOUSE INN. Directions: Located at the entrance to the park. **Season:** May through September. **Admission:** Free. **Telephone:** (716) 354-6095.

SENECA-IROQUOIS NATIONAL MUSEUM. Directions: Follow Route 17 to Exit 20. Bear right at end of ramp onto Broad Street. Museum will be almost immediately on your left. **Season:** Year round. **Admission:** Charged. **Telephone:** (716) 945-1738.

SALAMANCA RAIL MUSEUM. Directions: Located at 170 Main Street in Salamanca. **Season:** April through October. **Admission:** Free. **Telephone:** (716) 945-3133.

Chautauqua

T he winding streets and pathways, lined with gingerbread-trimmed Victorian houses, hearken back to the late 19th century. There are few cars to disturb the peace, only bikers and walkers. Trees bend over the narrow lanes, and window boxes and dooryard gardens brim with color. Children in bathing suits toss a frisbee. The trill of a flute floats through the air. Over here an artist works at an easel, and over there a young couple sits in the shade reading. The raised voices of animated conversation pierce the silence. A jogger bounces by, carrying a violin case. Welcome to **Chautauqua Institution.**

At first glance, it feels as though you've stepped back in time, but soon you'll realize that this unusual tableau is actually a backdrop designed to encourage animated exploration of contemporary ideas. Chautauqua is unlike any other destination in this book. It is a self-contained community, an ideal place for a brief or prolonged vacation. You are welcome to visit for a day, but most daytrippers find themselves returning year after year, lingering longer and longer. Once acquired, the Chautauqua habit is hard to shake.

Chautauqua Institution was founded in 1874 to meet the needs of Sunday School teachers. It began as the Chautauqua Sunday School Assembly, but from the beginning the idea was to cultivate religion through education. Although rooted in Christianity, Chautauqua is open to and well serves all who wish to come. Dr. John Heyl Vincent, a co-founder, once defined the Chautauqua mission as "self-improvement in all our faculties, for all of us through all time, for the greatest good of all people." Today the Institution calls itself "A Summertime Center for the Arts, Education, Religion, and Recreation." That's a pretty hefty claim, but, once you become acquainted with the scope and quality of the program, you'll see that Chautauqua makes good on it.

Most first-timers visit for the day. Most repeaters remain a week, a month, or the whole summer. At the height of the season, upwards of 12,000 people take part in the daily programs and activities at the Institution. To get an idea of what that means, we'll give you a run-down of the highlights of the summer programs. To begin with, there's the Chautauqua Symphony Orchestra, which offers more

Dr. Vincent defined the Chautauqua mission as "self-improvement in all our faculties, for all of us through all time, for the greatest good of all people."

Ballet is only one of many performing arts that flourish throughout the summer at the Chautauqua Institution.

than 20 concerts. The Chautauqua Opera presents operas in English, featuring principal singers from well-known companies. Visiting dance companies and a variety of musicians, including popular jazz and folk artists, perform in the 6,000-seat amphitheater. In a recent season, the Conservatory Theatre Company presented innovative productions of plays by writers varying from Bertolt Brecht to Tennessee Williams, Dylan Thomas to Carlo Goldoni. The lecture schedule includes appearances by outstanding figures in science, literature, and social and political affairs. Each week of the season is keyed to a particular theme (for example, World Peace, Health, and Wholeness; Business and Economics; or National Affairs, Humanities, and the Arts), which is reflected in lectures and seminars.

Pause in the amphitheater to listen to an orchestra rehearsal, or attend a creative writing workshop.

On arriving at Chautauqua Institution, you'll park your car before entering the enclosed grounds. Admission to Chautauqua is by gate ticket. This ticket admits you to the amphitheater and to most other events held on the grounds, with the exception of plays and operas requiring reserved seats. The day we visited, we listened to a famous theologian deliver a lecture in the open-air Hall of Philosophy, paused in the amphitheater to listen to an orchestra rehearsal, bought some homemade preserves at a sale sponsored by the Bird, Tree, and Garden Club, and attended a creative writing symposium. In between, we explored the attractive cluster of shops on the grounds and took a swim. In the early evening, we took a narrated bus tour of Chautauqua Institution.

Chautauqua is ideal for a family vacation, incorporating the very best elements of summer camp with an opportunity for families to enjoy spending time together. A complete program of activities is offered for children from 2½ years old to college age. For adults, the Summer Schools offer over a hundred workshops and courses of various lengths, with registration throughout the season. Courses at the School of Special Studies run the gamut from interior decorating to computers, foreign languages to soaring and gliding. There are also four separate schools in the fine and performing arts that bring professional faculty together with talented students on the verge of commencing their own careers. All this creates an atmosphere charged with intellectual and artistic energy, where visitors of all ages and abilities explore and expand on their own talents and interests in the company of a fascinating mix of people.

The community is located on the edge of Chautauqua Lake, and you'll want to explore the 63 miles of shoreline. Canoes and sailboats are available (more about them in a minute), or you can simply take a relaxing cruise on the *Gadfly III.* There are 1¼-hour and two-hour excursions scheduled throughout the week. Your captain offers observations about the flora, fauna, and architectural styles you encounter, and shares stories about local history, including anecdotes from the steamboat era.

The **Chautauqua Sports Club** offers facilities for shuffleboard, lawn bowling, horseshoes, and other activities. The club also holds exercise classes and organizes basketball, volleyball, and softball games. This is the place where you can rent those canoes and sailboats we mentioned. Week-long and season memberships can be purchased, and weekend participation can be arranged for some activities. In addition, Chautauqua Institution has an 18-hole golf course overlooking the lake There are also eight tennis courts, and lessons are available. Add to this three public beaches within the grounds — one just for children — and you begin to get an idea of the importance of recreation. Good fishing is also part of the fun, particularly during muskie season, which starts in mid-June.

CHAUTAUQUA INSTITUTION

Many of the charming houses on the Chautauqua grounds rent to summer guests, and visitors have a wide variety of options.

Since you will probably not be bringing your car into Chautauqua, you might want to consider renting a bicycle. One-, three-, five-, and ten-speed models are available from **Chautauqua Bike Rentals** by the hour, day, or week. Tandems and side-by-sides are also on hand if you want to try something a little out of the ordinary. If you bring along your own bike, you'll have to register it (small fee charged) with the Chautauqua Police Department.

If you are already hooked on the Chautauqua idea, you should send for information on accommodations. Houses within the community are individually owned, and many property owners rent out rooms or run guesthouses. Apartments and cottages are also available. In addition, there are several lovely hotels and inns to choose from, some of which offer package plans incorporating gate ticket, parking, meals, and lodgings. At Chautauqua you'll enjoy a self-contained vacation with a smorgasbord of options right at your doorstep.

At Chautauqua you'll enjoy a self-contained vacation with a smorgasbord of options right at your doorstep.

ACCESS

CHAUTAUQUA. To reach Chautauqua, follow Route 17 west (Southern Tier Expressway) to Exit 8 at Stow. Follow Route 394 north.

CHAUTAUQUA INSTITUTION. Directions: The main entrance and parking area are located on Route 394 in Chautauqua. **Season:** Most programs run from the end of June to the end of August. **Admission:** Charged. **Telephone:** (716) 357 6200.

GADFLY III. Directions: Boat departs from the bell tower dock at the Chautauqua Institution. No Chautauqua gate fee required; ask main gate attendant for boat pass. **Season:** Late June through August. **Admission:** Charged. **Telephone:** (716) 753-2753.

CHAUTAUQUA SPORTS CLUB. Directions: Located on the grounds of the Chautauqua Institution. **Season:** Late June through August. **Admission:** Charged. **Telephone:** (716) 357-6281.

CHAUTAUQUA BIKE RENTALS. Directions: Call ahead or inquire at main gate. **Season:** Late June through August. **Admission:** Rental fees charged. **Telephone:** (716) 357-5444.

For further information on Chautauqua Institution, including lodging suggestions and room and board packages on the grounds, write to Chautauqua Institution, Box 1095, Chautauqua, N.Y. 14722. Request the Visitors' Guide/Accommodations Directory and/or the Summer Schools Catalog.

Niagara Falls

NEW YORK POWER AUTHORITY

Why is Niagara Falls such a popular tourist attraction? One picture says it all.

Best known as the honeymoon capital of the United States, Niagara Falls continues to be a favorite vacation spot for families and older travelers as well as for newlyweds. We originally debated including Niagara Falls in this book; it's so well known, we reasoned, that there won't be anything new to say. And yet, we argued with ourselves, you don't skip Notre Dame when you visit Paris just because everyone goes there. As a matter of fact, the reason a particular destination is so popular might just be that it's also very special. So we went to check out Niagara Falls, just to see. . . . What we discovered is that not only are the falls themselves spectacular, but that there is also a lively array of activities to enjoy, some well known and others a bit more obscure.

Begin by visiting the falls themselves. The American Falls are 180 feet high with a brink of 1,100 feet. The Canadian Horseshoe Falls are 170 feet high, but over twice as wide with a brink of 2,500 feet, or nearly half a mile. To get a good view, you'll enter the **Niagara Reservation State Park,** a 200-acre preserve designed in the late 19th century by landscape architect Frederick Law Olmsted. Within the park, you can stand near the brink of the American Falls on Prospect Point. For a bird's-eye view of the falls, ride the elevator to the top of the **New York State Observation Tower.** If the sun is shining, you'll see rainbows arching over the spray at the base of the falls as the water thunders down. Then take the elevator down to the bottom of the falls where there are paths to walk.

Here at the base you can take a ride on one of the *Maid of the Mist* boats. The original *Maid of the Mist,* a wooden-hulled, coal-fired steamboat, was launched in 1846. Her descendants are a team of four steel diesel-powered boats. The half-hour cruise takes you in front of the American Falls and into the basin of the Canadian Falls. As you step aboard the green and white boat, you'll be handed a floor-length rubber raincoat. Put it on, and don't forget the hood! It's not a question of getting just a little wet. As the boat plows through the foamy swirls, you can get genuinely soaked. Think about that before casually pulling out your camera. Also, there were small children aboard the day we traveled on the *Maid,* and while some of them appeared to find the trip exciting, others clearly would rather have been somewhere else.

As you look up from the deck of the *Maid* the falls appear to be cascading from the sky. The captain entertains the passengers with anecdotes, providing both French and English narration. It seems the boats got their name from an Indian princess who was sent over the falls in a canoe as a sacrifice; it is said her spirit still roams in the caves behind the falls. More recently, a seven year old fell overboard in a boating accident and was washed over the falls and rescued by a *Maid of the Mist* boat.

An Indian princess was sent over the falls in a canoe as a sacrifice; it is said her spirit still roams in the caves behind the falls.

The water, which if fully harnessed would provide 12 million horsepower, comes from four of the Great Lakes and flows into the fifth one, Lake Ontario. From there it passes through the St. Lawrence Seaway and on into the Atlantic Ocean. And although the boat rides and other special activities are restricted to warm weather months, Niagara Falls is dramatic at any time of year. The falls are illuminated every evening, but from Thanksgiving through the end of December, they are lit up with thousands of colored lights.

Another way to get a close-up of the falls is to take the **Cave of the Winds** trip on Goat Island, which separates the American Falls from the Canadian Horseshoe Falls and which is accessible by foot from Prospect Point. You'll be given a raincoat and then you'll step into an elevator going down. When you get out, your guide will lead you through a small tunnel to the network of wooden walkways that clings to the base of Bridal Veil Falls. When you reach the Hurricane Deck, you'll be just 25 feet from the plummeting water. If you don't like boat rides, this is a good way to get your fair share of mist.

A pleasant way to get an overview of the Niagara Reservation is to buy a ticket for the **Viewmobile.** The open tractor trains circle the park at frequent intervals, and the drivers deliver a preset narration. You can get off and reboard at your leisure. The route originates near Prospect Point (but you can purchase a ticket and begin your tour at any of the five stops).

The Viewmobile crosses the Niagara River via the Goat Island bridges, passing over tiny Green Island and continuing on to Goat Island, large by comparison, measuring one-half mile in length and a quarter of a mile across. The Viewmobile driver explains that the island owes its name to an 18th-century farmer who moved his goats here by raft in order to escape ravaging wolves on the mainland.

You can get off at the first stop on Goat Island and climb to Luna Island for a dramatic close-up of Bridal Veil Falls. This is also the place to get off if you want to take the Cave of the Winds tour. The Viewmobile's next stop is at Terrapin Point. Here a path leads to the edge of Horseshoe Falls, where 100,000 cubic feet of water race over the brink every second. (Now how do they know that for sure?) Then it's on to the Three Sister Islands, which are connected by footbridges. You actually get right out over the rapids.

The Viewmobile's last stop is at the heliport, where **Huessler Air Service** offers five-minute spins up over the falls in a helicopter that looks like a plastic bubble with a propeller on top. Two adults can go up together, or three children, or an adult and two kids, just so long as everyone's combined weight stays under 400 pounds. From here the Viewmobile leaves Goat Island and returns to Prospect Point.

You'll probably want to spend a few hours in the park. There are places where you can buy refreshments, but we think it's more fun to bring along a picnic to eat near the rapids. Not to mention more economical — something to keep in mind,

For a bird's-eye view of the famous falls, visit the New York State Observation Tower.

since most of the activities in the park carry fairly steep fees. If you want to visit on a pennypincher's budget, keep in mind that there is no fee for entering the Niagara Reservation on foot and exploring to your heart's content. You can avoid the parking fee by leaving your car in the free garage at the Rainbow Centre, an enclosed shopping mall located just a block from the falls. The sign outside says "Free Falls Parking," so you don't even need to feel guilty about doing this.

If you do park here, be sure to take a look at the **Wintergarden,** a multistory glass enclosure adjoining the mall. You'll find tables and benches set out along elevated walkways and down near the fountain on the ground floor level. Settle down and take a break among the tropical plants, or make yourself comfortable while you feast on the food you purchased at the take-out stands clustered near the mall entrance to the garden.

To round out your visit to Niagara Falls, we suggest stops at two museums, both within walking distance of the Niagara Reservation. The **Schoellkopf Geological Museum** documents the formation of the dramatic waterfalls, a story that stretches back five million years. It all began with a great glacier that covered the region with ice, sometimes 3,000 feet thick. Exhibits and a multiscreen theater presentation illustrate the formation of the Great Lakes, the natural phenomenon of progressive erosion, and more. The museum overlooks the Niagara Gorge, and during the summer months staff members offer a variety of guided walks along the rim and down to the edge of the Niagara River, as well as to the base of the falls themselves.

The other museum is **The Turtle — The Native American Center for the Living Arts,** where you can see handsome collections of Iroquois artifacts. The turtle is honored by native Americans as one of the oldest life forms and as a symbol of the earth itself. Since prehistoric times, it has endured relatively unchanged. According to Indian legend, the earth was created on the back of a gigantic turtle. This huge "turtle island" spawned many groups of people, and the Indians honored the turtle through their art and ceremonies. This new museum is built in the shape of its namesake.

Here you will enter the world of the Houdenosaunee, also known as "the people of the long house" and "the Six Nations Iroquois people." This extensive exhibit focuses on the daily habits and social customs of the Houdenosaunee. We learn

In Indian folklore, the world was created on the back of a gigantic turtle.

Live dance demonstrations at The Turtle are one way to get acquainted with the Iroquois peoples and their heritage.

that their diet included 15 kinds of corn and 14 types of peas and beans, as well as the pond lily, sassafras bark, cattails, and fungi. They were known as the woodland Indians, and all of their spiritual and physical needs were satisfied by the fields, forests, and lakes and the creatures that inhabited them. From the wolves they learned to hunt in groups for the benefit of their families and from the heron they learned how to use fish to fertilize crops. Through the use of costumed mannequins and displays of household items like beaded pouches, musical instruments, jewelry baskets, and dolls, we get a real feeling for the Houdenosaunee.

Other special features at the museum include the live Iroquois dance demonstrations, which are held daily from late May to early September, and the Turtle Gallery Restaurant, which offers several traditional Indian dishes. The craft shop offers a fabulous collection of handmade items like wooden ladles with turtles carved into the handles and Mohawk pottery, along with original paintings.

To sum it all up, Niagara Falls is still well worth a visit. Traditional attractions like the *Maid of the Mist* tours blend well with newer ones like The Turtle, while Mother Nature continues to produce a round-the-clock first-rate show, just as she's done for thousands of years.

NIAGARA FALLS. To reach Niagara Falls, the state park area, follow I-90 (New York State Thruway) to Exit N-21; then follow Route 420 in the direction of the Rainbow Bridge.

NIAGARA RESERVATION STATE PARK. Directions: Route 420 will bring you to the parking lot for the park. **Season:** Year round. **Admission:** Parking fee. **Telephone:** (716) 278-1770.

NEW YORK STATE OBSERVATION TOWER. Directions: Located within the state park. **Season:** Year round. **Admission:** Small fee for elevator. **Telephone:** (716) 278-1770.

MAID OF THE MIST. Directions: Ticket booth is located in the state park. Boats depart from the base of the Observation Tower. **Season:** Mid-May to late October. **Admission:** Charged. **Telephone:** (716) 284-4233.

CAVE OF THE WINDS. Directions: Purchase tickets on Goat Island in the state park. **Season:** Mid-May to late October. **Admission:** Charged. **Telephone:** (716) 284-8897.

VIEWMOBILE. Directions: Ticket booth is located in the state park. **Season:** Mid-May through late October. **Admission:** Charged. **Telephone:** (716) 282-0028.

HUESSLER AIR SERVICE. Directions: Located on Goat Island in the state park. **Season:** May through the end of October. **Admission:** Charged. **Telephone:** (716) 282-6964.

WINTERGARDEN. Directions: Located in the Rainbow Mall complex, across from the main state park parking area. **Season:** Year round. **Admission:** Free. **Telephone:** (716) 278-8196.

SCHOELLKOPF GEOLOGICAL MUSEUM. Directions: From state park parking area, follow Robert Moses State Parkway to museum, which is located on state parkland. (There is also a footpath to the museum beginning at Prospect Point near the American Falls.) **Season:** Year round. **Admission:** Token fee from Memorial Day through Labor Day; free the rest of the year. **Telephone:** (716) 278-1780.

THE TURTLE — THE NATIVE AMERICAN CENTER FOR THE LIVING ARTS. Directions: Located at 25 Rainbow Mall, a three-minute walk from the main state park parking area. **Season:** Year round. **Admission:** Charged. **Telephone:** (716) 284-4867.

For lodging and restaurant suggestions, contact the Niagara Falls Convention and Visitors Bureau, 345 Third Street, Niagara Falls, N.Y. 14303. **Telephone:** (716) 278-8010.

North of Niagara

Millions of travelers make their way to Niagara Falls each year, and most of them head for home after admiring the world-famous falls and the attractions that cluster nearby. We think they're missing something. Take a day to head up north of Niagara and you'll see what we mean. Less geared toward the tourist trade, this area has much to offer the visitor who prefers to avoid crowds. As an added bonus, this cluster of places to visit offers some real bargains in unusual and free (or low-cost) vacation activities.

At the **Niagara Power Project Visitors' Center,** also known as Power Vista, you'll learn how the Niagara River has been harnessed to produce electricity. Power Vista is arranged in two connected buildings. The first contains the Hall of Energy, which houses displays showing how man converts natural energy into forms of energy he can use. There is even a visitor-operated water display that illustrates the principles involved in three early methods of using water power: the water pump, the water wheel, and the Archimedean screw.

Then take an escalator ride that carries you up to an overpass, crossing Route 104 and the Robert Moses Parkway. You'll end up in the Observation Building, where you'll enter the Niagara Museum of Power and Industry. Using pictures, tape recordings, and a large illuminated map, exhibits explain the geological development and the history of the falls, from 10,224 B.C. (the last glacial activity) to the present. Here you can take a look at the "Honeymoon Capital of the World" as depicted on a mutascope. A predecessor of motion pictures, this hand-cranked device uses flipping cards to convey movement as young couples kiss and cavort by the falls. There are also videos of Niagara, then and now, interspersed with comments made by famous people who came to visit and admire. As Oscar Wilde once observed, "The wonder would be if the water did not fall." In the film area, consisting of three theaters, visitors can activate presentations focusing on various aspects of the construction and operation of the Niagara Power Project and on other energy-related subjects. There is also a demonstration stage where live presentations are given.

In short, a visit to the power center is one of those all-too-rare travel bargains, particularly for

Take a look at the "Honeymoon Capital of the World" as depicted on an instrument called a mutascope.

Alien, Inca, or ancient Greek? None of the above, but a resident artist modeling his handiwork at Artpark.

families. There is no admission charge, and yet you are treated to a first-class science museum with lots of visitor-involving exhibits. Don't forget to stop by the observation deck on the top floor before completing your visit.

Continuing north, you'll soon come to Lewiston, home of **Artpark,** another splendid travel bargain. Other than a small parking fee, you won't have to pay a cent to enjoy the lively daytime schedule of workshops, demonstrations, and performances held in this 200-acre park throughout the summer. The unusual state park is a mecca for contemporary artists, who gather here to develop new works and to share their ideas, techniques, and accomplishments with park visitors. Most programs are housed along a sprawling network of broad, elevated boardwalks (called "the El"), embellished with a log cabin, a silo, and other unexpected nooks and crannies.

The day we wandered in, a group of young children was hard at work constructing books about themselves in the mirrored "Kids' Space." Lots of folks were snacking on tabouli, Polish sausages, and ice cream sundaes at the tables and chairs by the ArtEl Eatery. Close to a hundred kids and grown-ups grunted and groaned as they tried to duplicate the moves explained in a live karate demonstration. In the Under-the-El workshop, a bunch of kids signed up for a scavenger hunt. Older visitors watched cooking demonstrations in the Log Cabin Kitchen and wandered in and out of a series of craft shops, watching artists at work on projects as diverse as terra cotta vessels and hand-painted floorcloths. In the Artpark Store, an elegant space with a brick floor and a high ceiling that feels more like a gallery than a store, shoppers admired hand-crafted pieces, some made by Artpark artists.

The performing arts are also very much a part of the scene here. Storytellers, musicians, acrobats, actors, and mimes appear frequently in the daytime. At night, the 2,300-seat theater hosts musicals, concerts, and dance performances, featuring performers like The National Ballet of Canada, the Buffalo Philharmonic Orchestra, and Ella Fitzgerald. You'll need to purchase tickets for these events.

One menu includes summer soup and crabmeat salad, while another calls for spicy shrimp cocktail, cold barbecued sirloin, and French potato salad.

If you plan to attend an evening performance, instead of going out to dinner treat yourself to an elegant alternative — a catered picnic at Artpark. All you have to do is give **Artpark Catering Service** three days' notice. Now this isn't going to be any ordinary al fresco feed; when you order, you'll select from one of eight different menus. One offering includes summer soup and crabmeat salad, while another calls for spicy shrimp cocktail, cold barbecued sirloin steak, and French potato salad. Both come with raw vegetables, cheeses, French bread, and homemade dessert. Coffee, or hot or iced tea, is always included in the package price, and wine can be ordered at an additional cost. It's not just the menu, though, that makes this picnic unusual — it's the way the food is presented. Your meal will come prettily packed in a basket, complete with mints, fresh flowers, silverware, and linens. And you don't have to eat on the ground. A table will be set aside for your convenience. All picnics are prepared for a minimum of two people.

If you'd like to explore Lewiston proper, stop in at the tiny **Museum of the Historical Society of Lewiston,** located in a former church built in 1835. Take a look inside the re-created storefront depicting Oliver Grace's Bookstore and Printing Office. The pulpit is set up to represent a large hearth, with displays of 19th-century cooking implements like a large wooden sausage stuffer and domestic artifacts like a tin bathtub complete with seat. You'll also see old documents relating to the town's history and a map, with photographs attached, showing the locations of present-day houses that date back to the 1830s. Take a walk along Center Street and you'll be able to find some of them.

A bit north of Lewiston, you'll come to **Joseph Davis State Park,** a pleasant place to spend a few hours outside. The big draw here is the swimming complex, which features a double Olympic-size swimming pool, a separate diving pool, a wading pool, and a large sunning lawn. There is lots of playground equipment spread about the grounds, including slides, seesaws, roundabouts, and swings. Bring along a couple of frisbees and try a round of disc golf. There are 18 different disc poles, and the player whose saucer makes contact with all of them in the fewest throws is the winner. Ask for a score-card and a set of rules in the bathhouse office, where you can also pick up a leaflet that provides information on the park nature trail. In the winter, the park is open for cross-country skiing.

Bring along a couple of frisbees and try a round of disc golf. The player whose saucer makes contact with all 18 poles in the fewest tries is the winner.

History buffs will want to continue a few miles north to **Old Fort Niagara,** located in Fort Niagara State Park. Strategically placed at the mouth of the Niagara River, the fort controlled access to the Great Lakes during Colonial times. Its strategic value diminished with the completion of the Erie Canal in 1825, yet it remained an active military post into the early 20th century. Originally built by the French, the fort has at different times also been held by British and American troops, each of whom sought the support of a fourth nation, the powerful Iroquois Confederacy. Different parts of the fort were constructed between 1726 and 1872, and while many are still intact today, others have disappeared. Archeologists can often be seen at work on the grounds, continuing to search for pieces of the past.

The "French Castle" at Old Fort Niagara, as it looks today.

You will be given a guided tour to 12 points of interest within the fort. In the guard tower, a costumed interpreter explains that about 14 men lived here, sharing common bunks, and that each spent every third day on guard duty. That meant remaining in uniform for 24 hours, spending two hours on guard, four hours off, around the clock. He'll show you the components of his uniform, including the long woolen hose held up by garter belts and canvas gaiters worn over his shoes. On a table in the center of the room you'll see the haversack each man used for important personal items (like soap), along with early board games like Fox and Geese and Nine Man Morris, used to while away the hours.

Each man spent every third day on guard duty: two hours on guard, four hours off, around the clock.

The oldest, largest building you'll visit is the French Castle, constructed in 1726. Under terms of their agreement with the Iroquois, the French built a stone "House of Peace" as a trading post, surrounding it with a simple wooden stockade. Trading post or not, the stone building was made to shelter a garrison of 60 men; storehouses, a powder magazine, and even a well were constructed within its walls. Twenty years later it was enlarged, with the addition of barracks, more storehouses, and a bakery. In time, the castle was used more and more as officers' quarters.

Special events take place frequently each day. We saw members of the King's 8th Regiment, in their red coats and high furry hats, shoulder and recover their bayonets in quick order to the beat of a drum. "It was the goal of the British army," we were told, "to move as one well-oiled machine." As you walk about the grounds and in and out of the great stone buildings, you'll have no trouble transporting yourself back in time to the beginning of our nation's history.

ACCESS

NORTH OF NIAGARA. From Niagara Falls, follow the Robert Moses Parkway north (Route 18F).

NIAGARA POWER PROJECT VISITORS' CENTER. **Directions:** From Buffalo, take Interstate 190 north to last U.S. exit, where you pick up Route 104 (Ridge Road). Travel west on Route 104 to Visitors' Center. **Season:** Year round. **Admission:** Free. **Telephone:** (716) 285-3211, ext. 6660.

ARTPARK. Directions: Located in Lewiston, seven miles north of Niagara Falls. Follow the Robert Moses Parkway (Route 18F) north to Route 104 (Ridge Road). Follow

Route 104 west; at cloverleaf, follow signs to Lewiston, via Center Street. Turn left on Portage Road and continue on to park entrance. **Season:** Late June through early September. **Admission:** Parking fee charged. **Telephone:** (716) 745-3377.

ARTPARK CATERING SERVICE. Directions: Picnics are picked up at the theater bar in Artpark. **Season:** Late June through early September. **Admission:** Fees charged for picnics. **Telephone:** (716) 278-8010.

MUSEUM OF THE HISTORICAL SOCIETY OF LEWISTON. Directions: Located at corner of Niagara and Plain streets in Lewiston. **Season:** June 1 through September 1, Wednesday through Sunday afternoons. **Admission:** Free. **Telephone:** None.

JOSEPH DAVIS STATE PARK. Directions: Follow the Robert Moses Parkway (Route 18F) north about 13 miles from Niagara Falls. **Season:** Year round. **Admission:** Charged. **Telephone:** (716) 285-8521.

OLD FORT NIAGARA. Directions: From Lewiston, follow the Robert Moses Parkway (Route 18F) north to Fort Niagara State Park. Signs in park will direct you to the fort. **Season:** Year round. **Admission:** Charged. **Telephone:** (716) 745-7611.

For lodging and restaurant suggestions, contact the Convention and Visitors Bureau, 300 Fourth Street, P.O. Box 786, Niagara Falls, N.Y. 14303. **Telephone:** (716) 278-8010.

Index

About the Author

Harriet Webster is the author of *Trips for Those Over 50,*
Coastal Daytrips in New England, Favorite Weekends in New
England, and *Favorite Short Trips in New York State.* She
wrote *Winter Book,* and *Going Places,* two nonfiction
children's books. She's also the author of *Family Secrets:*
How Telling and Not Telling Affect Our Children.

Her articles have been published in *McCall's, Made-*
moiselle, Family Circle, Parents, Working Mother, Better
Homes and Gardens, Seventeen, Women's World, Bride's,
and *Yankee.* Her travel stories have appeared in *Ameri-*
cana, The Boston Globe, The Christian Science Monitor,
Newsday, and *Boston* magazine. She lives in Gloucester,
Massachusetts.